Virginia Waite

SARDINIA

B. T. Batsford Ltd., London

To Frankie with love

First published 1977
© Virginia Waite 1977
ISBN 0 7134 0039 0

Printed in Great Britain by
The Pitman Press Ltd., Bath
for the publishers B. T. Batsford Ltd.,
4 Fitzhardinge Street, London W1H 0AH

Contents

	List of Illustrations	6
	Map of Sardinia	7
	Acknowledgments	8
1	Introduction	9
2	Festivals	22
3	Cagliari	39
4	Province of Cagliari	56
5	Oristano	80
6	Province of Oristano	87
7	Sassari	94
8	Province of Sassari	100
9	Nuoro	138
10	Province of Nuoro	144
	Index	166

List of Illustrations

Opposite page

1 and 2 Traditional dress for the Cavalcada Procession
on Ascension Day at Sassari   16

3 CAGLIARI. Città vecchia   17

4 and 5 CAGLIARI. The Procession for the Festival of
Sant'Efisio on May 1st   32

6 CAGLIARI. The Arogonese-Gothic crypt and cloisters
of the church of San Domenico   33

7 Porto Pino   48

8 Cap Boi   48

9 Nora excavations near Pula in Cagliari Province   49

10 Su Nuraxi excavations   49

11 NUORO   64

12 OLIENA in Nuoro Province   65

13 Cala Gonone in Nuoro Province   96

14 Mountain scenery in Nuoro Province   97

15 SILANUS (near Macomer): Chiesetta di Santa
Serbana   97

16-18 Three Island Churches: Tratalias; the Cathedral at
Oristano; the Cathedral at Sassari   112

19 SASSARI. Traditional costume for the Ascension
Day Procession   113

20 Costa Smeralda   144

21 Porto Rafael, Palau   144

22 Porto Cervo, Arzachena (Sassari Province)   145

23 The countryside outside Bosa (Sassari Province)   160

24 La Maddalena, Cala Lunga (Sassari Province)   161

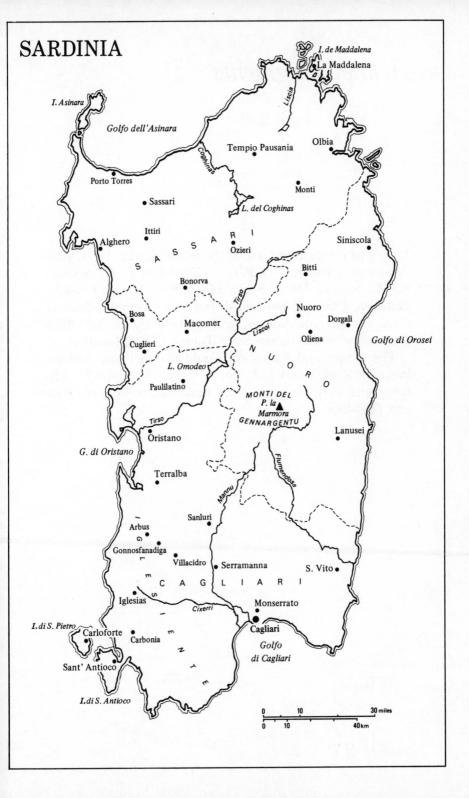

Acknowledgments

My grateful thanks are due to the following: Dr. Piras, Ente Provinciale Turismo (E.P.T.), Cagliari; Dr. G. Solinas, E.P.T., Sassari; Dr. E. Bacchiddu, E.P.T., Nuoro; Giuliana Bellasich, Ufficio Pubblicata della Costa Smeralda; Beatrice Cook for her translations; and particularly to Mr. John Greenwood of the Italian State Tourist Office, London.

The author and Publishers would like to thank Barbara Wace for illustrations 1, 2, 4-6, 8-10, 14, 15, 19 and 23. The remainder were courtesy of the Italian State Tourist Office and Foto-Enit.

1 Introduction

Sardinia gives the impression of being several different countries, although it is small enough to drive from one end to the other in a day. It manages this by a mixture of geographical, historical and linguistic factors, all of which can fool the absent-minded visitor into believing he must be somewhere else. Surely the people are speaking Spanish, not Italian? They certainly are in the northern port of Alghero which was a Spanish colony. Meanwhile up in the mountains the keen Latin scholar will get on famously, and indeed to speak Italian there can actually be a disadvantage, for the wary nomadic shepherds in these remote areas will then mistake you for an 'enemy', which to them is anyone from the mainland. Their Latin heritage dates from Roman times.

Down in the south, North Africa appears to have drifted 120 miles and attached itself to two Sardinian islands, complete with mosque-like churches and regional dishes such as couscous, for here the first settlers came from Tunisia. Such complexities can make for a bewildering initial encounter, until you realise that the typical Sard sub-divides into dozens of different typical Sards and that each area, with the highest patriotism, sees itself in a specially privileged position, as 'an island within an island'.

One reason for these distinct population divisions is the topography of the island. The coastal areas were most vulnerable to attack and subjugation, hence their dialects reflecting the conquerors. The central mountain range rising to just over 6,000 feet was the refuge against those attacks and remains an impenetrable misty region. So it is no surprise that the early cave-dwelling Sards up here became expert guerillas – and still are today, to the frustration of the Italian carabinieri trying to combat the banditry that has been endemic since Roman times.

The Romans concentrated on the two aspects of Sardinia that could bring them revenue: agriculture, in which the rolling cornfields of the Campidano plain became the Imperial granary of Rome; and mining, in which they monopolised the market by the simple expedient of prohibiting anyone connected with the industry other than themselves, from visiting the island. Both livelihoods flourish today, with expansion of farming between the two world wars through the reclamation of swamp land. To the early precious metals of silver, gold, lead and copper have been added zinc, antimony, coal – providing Italy's only natural supply – and fluorspar, the most important source in Europe.

Economically, the most important post-war help the island has received from the mainland has come, as in Sicily, from the Italian Government development scheme, the Cassa per il Mezzogiorno, with money being pumped in for new businesses, training of workers and so on. Typically, though, the Sards themselves seem to remain fairly ungrateful for the hand-outs and complain that it is other people who get the money and the benefits. One of them put it like this: 'We still feel oppressed and believe it is the continentals – that is those from Italy – who get the loans and the subsequent profits.' Furthermore, the Sards are also divided on the thorny question of who is being aided and there is continuing friction between the mountain shepherds, who point to the plains farmers as the recipients, and the lowland folk who are equally convinced that the lucky ones are the land-owning uplanders.

Lack of work has ever been a problem and has resulted in migration to Germany and the United States. Now, in at least one area – the Costa Smeralda, the international luxury playground established by the Aga Khan and his friends on the north-east coast – the immigrants are coming home. The barren region they left, capable of supporting only a few shepherds and fishermen, has moved into the twentieth century with piped water and all amenities, including jobs.

The other barrier to work in the early days was malaria, the disease brought in by the Carthaginians. The campaign to eradicate it was organised by the United Nations Relief and Rehabilitation Association, under the sponsorship of the Rockefeller Foundation of the United States. Teams of Americans, Britons and Sards literally bathed the island's stagnant water and houses with anti-malarial disinfectant over a period of six years. Today the fading D.D.T. stamp can be seen everywhere, and though there is no longer a population of yellow weakened faces, the older women continue to drape their headscarves across their mouths, the ancient precaution against the disease.

It was during the malaria campaign that Sardinia gained its current degree of autonomy, with a junta that handles almost all domestic policies, though Italy controls custom and excise, railways, armed forces and most of the police. Each of the four provinces of Cagliari, Sassari, Nuoro and Oristano have an important say in administering their own areas, which is not only sensible but vital, as they cannot all necessarily understand each other's dialect and sometimes need to turn to Italian as a common tongue. More than 100 years ago an English barrister, John Warre Tyndale, who produced a meticulous three-volume survey of Sardinia, wrote: 'Italian is used in official transactions and by the higher classes; and with a knowledge of that language, Latin and Spanish, a stranger may soon understand the native tongue.'

This language mixture has not changed since, though without Tyndale's linguistic ability the native tongue is not easy to grasp. Logudorese means gold place and it is the nearest to pure Latin spoken in the north-west, with the disconcerting addition of Alghero's Spanish. In the mountains the dialect is Sardo, which any reincarnated Roman would understand. In the north-east the early Pisan domination has produced a sweet lilting language similar to that spoken in Tuscany, except that the archipelago nearby shows French influence from Corsica just across the water. The southern off-shore islands, on the other hand, derive their language from the Genoese.

Many Sards, as a consequence, speak better Italian than the Italians, because they have kept this second language pure and uncorrupt. To sum up a true Sard among the one and a half million of them is almost impossible. One marvellously partisan viewpoint describes them like this:

> The Sardinian has not possessed the social and political instinct of the vast community. His is the individual instinct which imperiously asserts his authority over the family group. In the family, the Sardinian is the undisputed head; outside the family relationship he is not prepared to admit the authority of a law alien to traditional and local custom.

It is a somewhat ornate summing-up of a character that quite simply believes in its own rightness. A small anecdote illustrates the theme. When a householder asked her gardener to plant the gladioli bulbs she had saved for this purpose from the previous year, he assured her they would never come up and put them in reluctantly. They did, but the triumph was short-lived. An identical argument ensued the following year because, as the gardener pointed out, the first success was a million-to-one chance and could never happen again.

The Sard belief that he alone knows the answer can lead to highly entertaining scenes. Before one of the island's famous festivals I was noting down costume detail, and when it came to the long sheepskin jacket worn by some of the men my interpreter confidently announced its name. He was immediately contradicted by the wearer of the jacket whose suggested name was, in turn, dismissed by others in the group. An animated argument began in which no definitive name for the garment was agreed upon. Tyndale, so many years ago, had the same problem, trying to identify an ancient site he was visiting. One peasant gave him the 'right' name, another passing by refuted it and produced a second, to be dismissed by a third peasant with yet another version.

Like me and the costume, Tyndale gave up and went on to describe what he actually saw, which was an example of quite the most interesting and unique aspect of Sardinia's history: the period from 1500 B.C. when the Proto-Sards lived on the island. Evidence of their occupation is overwhelming, yet not one word did they write down. Their settlements, of which there are still something like 7000, are called nuraghe, which could translate as height or habitation, both being equally applicable. Today's ruins show the visitor magnificent fortresses with truncated cones, which have lasted much longer than any Roman buildings, for the simple reason that they are built of blocks of basalt taken from extinct volcanoes and impervious to erosion or decay.

The central towers, most experts agree, were the defensive structure in which the inhabitants of the outlying village could take refuge in times of trouble. They were built, over a period of 1000 years, in the manner of the Egyptian pyramids, so that the stones were rolled up an earth ramp, the ramp going higher as the building did until it was finally, literally, unearthed from its surrounds. In addition to the nuraghe, there are from the same period, burial sites called Domus de Janas (witches' houses) – grottoes hollowed out of the rock face – and for collective burial, the Giants' Tombs; both types of construction contain corridors and chambers and have a rather sinister aspect, though they have no discernible links with their names.

Apart from the buildings, the Proto-Sards left behind their utensils – axes, arrows, ceramics and so on – plus one spectacular bonus: hundreds upon hundreds of bronze statuettes to tell the story of their lives, which are now safely displayed in the museums of Cagliari and Sassari. Exactly when the nuraghic peoples finally disappeared is not known, but certainly by the time of the Roman occupation the villages and fortresses had been either destroyed or buried and the inhabitants fled.

Sardinia is said to have been named after a Livyan called Sardus, though some historians claim it evolved from Sandaliota, meaning sandal, after its shape. What is not in dispute is that the Phoenicians established trading stations around 800 B.C. and founded colonies on the southern end of the island, attracted by the good anchorages and the need to find stop-over points on their seagoing routes. But it was the aggressive Carthaginians who first came up against the independent Sard spirit around 560 B.C. and found it took more than one attempt and much force to subdue the islanders.

These conquerors were anything but benevolent. They not only banished the remaining inhabitants from all the fertile areas, but propounded the severest penalties for anyone found growing anything. However, the Sards gained something from their tyrants. They learnt how to read and write, how to use money and how valuable land was. They also saw the horse for the first time, and experienced malaria, a not-so-convenient import. Although Rome and Carthage had originally been friendly, their relations changed to antagonism, which led to warfare on Sardinian soil and the victors moved in to take over in 238 B.C., making the island the first Roman province and Cagliari a port for the Roman fleet.

Their rule was hardly less severe than that of their predecessors and something like 150,000 Sards were slain or taken captive to Rome over a period of less than 150 years. They carried on agriculturally where the Carthaginians left off, and in this they were so successful that they had to build special granaries in Rome for receiving the island's corn. They also used Sardinia as a convenient dumping ground for exiles, among whom numbered 4000 Jews and Egyptians. The Sards retaliated by swooping down from their mountain caves in guerilla raids.

The general Roman opinion of the Sard was, naturally, uncomplimentary. Cicero described them as the most deceitful of nations, and it was even suggested that their two-faced approach was the origin of the phrase a sardonic smile. (In fact its derivation is rather less whimsical: the islanders mistook an inedible wild parsley for an edible version and the symptoms of eating it led to contraction of the face muscles into a grimace.)

About the only real benefit the Sards derived from the 700 year-long Roman occupation was the building of roads and bridges, some of which are still in use. Following the decline of the Roman Empire, Sardinia passed to new oppressors – the Vandals; briefly the Goths; and then the Byzantines who were, however, too far away to control events absolutely, which gave both the Saracens and the Lombards endless opportunities for raiding parties. None of these contenders seem to have had any real effect on the Sards who took two main steps to protect and advance themselves. In the ninth century they became a part of the Roman See, while, around the same time, they were busy organizing their own form of self-government with four giudice, or judges, of the island.

Although there are no records of the first elections, it is clear these early rulers were chosen from rich and influential people, and the vote – unusual for those days – was extended to the general populace. One theory was that the giudice evolved from a Byzantine viceroy who elected himself to the post in order to increase his powers as he was, conveniently, so far away from his bosses. Another is that during the invasions of the Saracens and Lombards the islanders rallied round their own leaders in various regions. Whatever the origin, the system of government lasted for something like 600 years, often limited in power by external events and by the fact that the giudice did not always rule in peaceful co-existence. There was also the trying intervention of the Pisans and the Genoese and it was the Pope, on the pretext of restoring law and order to the island, who 'invited' these contenders to invade Sardinia.

Actually the Pisans and Genoese did combine to get rid of the Saracens in 1022, but from then on fought each other, totally disregarding the Sards, for something like 300 years, though on a number of occasions they had to contend with the natives who, if it seemed they would benefit, offered to help one side or the other in return for continuing occupation of their lands and properties. When the Pisans fell out with the Pope towards the end of the thirteenth century, the Papal See reassumed its right to dispose of the island as it willed under the earlier allegiance of the Sards and transferred Sardinia to the Aragon crown.

It took the Aragonese almost a century to dominate the entire island, but once installed they were to remain for nearly 400 years, and again the rulers of Sardinia had no intention of improving the lot of the natives. Indeed in the vital port of Alghero they calmly banished the entire population and replaced it with their own Spanish colony. Nothing historically important happened for more than a couple of centuries, although the printing press was introduced and the university of Cagliari founded. The Jesuits arrived, and so did the Spanish Inquisition, which led to the expulsion of the Jews originally exiled here by the Romans.

The War of the Spanish Succession ended their domination and, by a treaty signed in London in the early eighteenth century, the island was handed to the Duke of Savoy who accepted the title of King of Sardinia, although his capital, Turin, was in Piedmont. By 1720 it was formally in the hands of the House of Savoy. The new Sardinian King, Vittorio Amadeo II, was in fact liked by the Sards and he did make a start on long-overdue reforms and a lifting of some of the oppressions.

But he reigned for only ten years before abdicating in favour of his son. Why he gave up the crown has never been made clear. It could have been that his turncoat dealings with France and Austria got out of hand; it could have been the constant threats of war; it could have been the loss of his queen and his re-marriage to an ambitious countess who had been maid-of-honour to his first wife. Certainly, the announcement in September 1730, came as a surprise not only to his ministers and court but to his daughter-in-law, the Princess of Piedmont, who became Queen while his son, Carlo Emanuele III, took over the kingship.

It was a decision Amadeo II came to regret and when his exile in Chambery began to bore him he made, under pressure from his new wife, a foolish and stupid attempt to recover his throne. These plans reached Carlo Emanuele and there followed difficult and emotional meetings between father and son, the older not aware that the younger knew of the plot. At one stage Amadeo even demanded his son's abdication. There could be only one end. Carlo Emanuele signed a warrant for his father's arrest. The old man died a couple of years later and his countess spent the rest of her life in a convent.

Once the treaty of Aix-la-Chapelle had been signed in 1748, ensuring peace in Italy, Carlo Emanuele III was able to devote himself to the affairs of his kingdom in Sardinia. He was the first man in that island's history who cared about his dominion, and actually set about improving the lot of the people. He was an austere, formal man, who not only reduced his personal expenses but appointed a commission to 'persuade' others to do the same. Although he was a strict man who demanded high standards, far from being resented, he was emulated by his court, while the idle aristocracy, probably for the first time in their lives, found that they became employed in civil positions when they were not fighting on the king's behalf.

Carlo Emanuele's attention, however, was by no means restricted to those of his own kind. His reduction of expenses enabled him to give generously – and he expected everyone else in a financially sound position to do likewise. He encouraged the arts and sciences; he was a meticulous and conscientious though not brilliant soldier; he extended and improved in many different areas – commerce, agriculture, education, judiciary, volunteer guard corps and so on; and he even tried to solve the bandit question by resettling depopulated areas. Stern, proud, aloof though he was, when he died in 1774 at the age of 72 after a rule lasting close to half a century, the Sards had every reason to be grateful to him.

The next golden age was not to come their way until the end of the monarchy, though to be fair to the succeeding Sardinian kings external circumstances were largely to blame for the ensuing disasters. The first of these 'circumstances' was Napoleon, who, in a sharp two-week campaign in 1793 annihilated the King of Sardinia's troops and deprived him of his arsenal, stores, most of his friends and most of his titles; the king died a few months later, in a state of bankruptcy. Even during his short reign the king's actions seemed to have been designed to antagonise the Sards, for he brought in the hated Piedmontese to run the administration, and it took a Sard rebellion before the king agreed that the islanders could have the right to elect their own officials. Typically, the

Sards fell out amongst themselves with this new freedom and perhaps it was partly their internal squabbles that led to the abdications of the next kings.

Two Aragonese brothers followed and ruled consecutively, until both abdicated leaving a third brother who managed to stay the course and at least made some attempt to help his people. The final monarch of the House of Savoy succeeded in 1831 and set about the abolition of feudalism. There were a series of royal proclamations and two decrees, one appointing a commission to decide exactly how much, in money or goods, the peasants should pay the barons, and the second an attempt to transfer land from lord to peasant.

It was an excellent theory, but one which for a number of years failed to produce its intended benefit; the peasants found themselves having to pay just as much if not more to the crown as they had done to the barons, added to which they were so much in debt that they were in no position to cease being serfs. In any case, they showed the Sard antagonism to any change. The control of the House of Savoy over the island's destiny ended with the formal unification of Sardinia with Italy in 1861.

So the Sards have had just over 100 years to become themselves, to rediscover their own character and independence, though in truth it has been only half buried during the centuries of invasions and rule by others. Two traits that have never altered are their courtesy and hospitality. The former, though, can have its drawbacks because with it comes an insistence on telling you what they think you want to know, rather than the precise truth. The young son of a kidnapped industrialist who had been murdered by his abductors was firmly told by the servants that his father had only been injured. He turned to his American mother to say: 'You, I know, will tell me the truth.'

Sard hospitality is rightly renowned and it is no use inviting one of them to lunch and expecting to pay for the meal. Equally, when visiting homes, the stranger will be passed from house to house like a fragile parcel, and the circuit can be endless. Old customs, though, are dying out. A decade ago girls and boys could only look at each other and not speak or write without their parents' permission. Now the youngsters may toe the line in their home town, but there is a good deal more flexibility when they are out of sight of their elders, and discotheques are nearly as common as elsewhere in Europe.

Courtship, however, is another matter. The young man's parents call upon the young girl's parents to give each other's permission for the couple to meet, and it is still vital that the prospective bridegroom provides a home, complete with furniture, before the wedding can take place, which is why you see so many younger brides of older men.

It is surprising in many ways that the traditional customs have lasted this long, for Sardinia is now most well connected to the outside world by air and sea. The exclusive Costa Smeralda is served by its own airline flying in to nearby Olbia, and there are two other international airports, Fertilia for Alghero and Sassari in the north, and Elmas for the capital, Cagliari, in the south, though there is one aspect of your arrival and departure at the latter which may surprise you.

Elmas airport, up until 1975, is only half-operating for much of the time, which means that flights are diverted without warning to the air force base at Decimomannu a half hour's drive away. The first inkling you get is after checking in your luggage and being handed a bus ticket. You discover there is not a plane in sight and, ominously, a long-distance coach is sitting outside. In fact it does not delay you much and at the base, in a converted hangar, is a temporary security check. Take-off does not take precedence over military jets. There is one other point of value to air travellers, particularly if there should be any delay when changing planes at Milan or Rome. The leg to Sardinia is an internal Alitalia domestic flight and so serves no refreshments whatsoever irrespective of the time of day. A cup of coffee and a sandwich while awaiting the connection is a wise precaution.

Motorists can bring in their cars by ferry to Cagliari from the Italian mainland, Sicily and Tunis; or to Porto Torres, Olbia and Arbatax from Italy; or to Santa Teresa di Gallura from Corsica. In addition there are local boats connecting Sardinia with its off-shore islands in the south, Sant'Antioco and San Pietro, and its northern archipelago centred upon La Maddalena. Local tourist offices will supply a handy timetable of all these, plus train and bus services. Do not, however, expect an up to date version. I arrived the day before a new one should have been available, it was not, and never became so. But it does not make too much difference because to turn up for a non-existent ferry merely means a 30-minute wait in the nearest cafe. An essential item is the three-part maps put out by the Italian Touring Club and available only in Italy or in London – not in Sardinia.

The climate is western Mediterranean, claiming nine months sunshine per year, but the mountains were still snow-covered in late May on my visit and the prevailing north-west maestrale was blowing, though this is much preferable to the hot sirocco from the south-east. One bonus for the visitor is that it does not matter where you begin. The historical mosaic – or perhaps maze would be a better word – does not require making a circuit in a particular order and you can choose those facets and regions of the island that interest you.

Perhaps it will be the craggy coastline, quite a lot of which is reachable only by boat, and a paradise for gogglers and skin-divers as well as yachtsmen who have several havens in amongst the treacherous rocks that thwarted early invading sailors. Those parts of the shore with beaches are moving fast into the twentieth century, but by comparison with some crowded Mediterranean coasts it is still spacious. A London barber, for instance, was rather disappointed with his sun, sand and sea Sardinian holiday, complaining that the island was not developed enough. If the coast hides its treasures, such as the spectacular grottoes, the interior is equally shy. Some of the mountain caves require an expedition to explore, which is why they made such excellent hideaways for the early Sards. Most holidaymakers, though, will be content to drive through, stopping at shepherd villages and experiencing some truly original food. Mountain hotels tend to open only between June and September. Luckily, this does not apply to the big cities, and if you wish to attend some of the island's most celebrated events you need to be there in May.

2 Festivals

To arrive in Sardinia on the eve of a festival is not only appropriate, but relatively common, for the island has made a speciality of them and you would be unlucky indeed to spend an entire holiday without running across at least one. A little guide book lists what it calls these manifestations, but warns that it has included only the most important. The list runs to seven pages and more than 40 events, ranging from the downright pagan to the devoutly religious.

There are still a few islanders who believe in magic, witches and enchantment. But even the most modern inhabitants are prepared to stretch a point by burning an effigy of the carnival king, and as this takes place in winter the villages light bonfires and bake fritters or cakes to hand out to spectators. Once converted to Catholicism, Sardinia has, over the centuries, gathered a very large number of Saints. Even if there are no relics and the Saint's story owes more to legend than to fact, the Sards have an endearing and deep belief, and in more than one church the grateful recipients of miracles leave gifts in thanks for their deliverance. Naturally, each and every Saint has his own day, with processions and rejoicing, though the religious base is invariably combined with fun and folklore.

Those villages which have been unable to raise a religious figure are by no means stuck for a festival idea. They turn to a celebration of their particular harvest, and that can be festivals of the sea, or festivals of the grape – there is a rash of these around September and October –

or a festival of almonds by the town which puts these nuts in its famous sweets. In the rare instances when there seems to be no reason whatsoever to hold a fiesta, firework displays, regattas, gastronomic fairs, handicraft shows and dare-devil horse-racing fill the gaps, all of which fit into the category of manifestations.

Nor are the Sards in the least bit parsimonious when it comes to the question of how long a festival should last. While some go on for a mere 24 hours, that is from shortly after dawn to well after midnight, others run for three or four days and there is a whole series in country churches which last for nine days, the pilgrims living alongside the while and combining the event with their annual holiday. In a little over a week I attended a trio of Sardinia's most celebrated events, starting in the island's capital with a famous Saint who is one of a number said to have been martyred under the Romans.

Sant'Efisio is credited with removing the plague from Cagliari in 1656, from which time the town authorities instituted a festival in thanksgiving to him. He is also said to be responsible for other remarkable feats, including the withdrawal of a French invasion in 1793, when he produced such a storm that the enemy fleet was forced to retreat. Today's ceremonies, the Sagra di Sant'Efisio, are a marvellous mixture of folklore and religion, of spectacle and fun, a grand bank holiday when everyone who can comes to the capital to see the procession.

A major feature of the parade are the traccas, decorated oxencarts, which assemble in a back street several hours before the start. Their most charming aspect is in the use of homely items for decoration. Bits of carpet provide drapery and seating; the 'Sunday best' lace tablecloth is used as a canopy with paper flowers stuck in it; a traditional carved wooden chest, usually a family heirloom, makes a fine back-end for the cart.

When it comes to the oxen, wearing brocade forehead cloths and bells, there is real originality. The animals stand amiably still while silver stars are stuck to their sides, their 'earrings' of gigantic bundles of coloured rags are adjusted, and their horns are embellished. This last is the key to the whole ensemble, and it is quite amazing how conducive oxen horns are to ornamentation. Take a couple of oranges, for instance, a neat slit in each, and stick them atop the horns. Take the table-runner from the sideboard and use it to cover the yoke. Swathe the horns with material. The varieties seem endless, particularly with paper flowers, sometimes used as a garland to link the horns, sometimes as an ornate cone atop each one. One lucky farmer lives close enough to bring fresh arum lilies and greenery to use as ornamentation.

It is not just animals and carts that are getting this pre-parade attention. Adjusting the human headgear is quite a ritual, be it the famed stocking cap worn by men or a delicate lace headdress. As one young man lifts his girl to her place on the cart he gently spreads out her long pleated skirt so that she becomes a part of the decoration. The riders, whose horses are breakfasting, stroll around, often carrying their refreshment with them, in the form of a small wooden barrel under one arm. Those who deem themselves to be absolutely ready walk proudly up and down, not just to be admired, but to meet friends they may not have seen for a year.

All of this takes several hours, and then there is the question of choosing a vantage point along the procession route. Following the crowd leads first into a horribly tawdry chapel with a fake grotto, and the procession in miniature, and then into Sant'Efisio's subterranean chapel, a dark sombre place reached by a steep narrow stairway. Out in the streets it is a warm Mediterranean day and spectators are lined several feet deep on the pavements with a friendly police force pleading in vain for people to shift just one step back. When the parade finally begins, within an hour or so of its advertised starting time, it becomes immediately apparent that oxen are a bonus, because they move at just the right dignified slow pace to enable everyone to get a good look.

The procession is headed by eight white horses whose policemen riders are wearing navy blue dress uniforms and Bonaparte black hats with red and blue plumes. They are the only ones who have actually dressed up for the occasion; everyone else is playing themselves, albeit in Sunday best. The carts are crammed with as many as 18 people, and though banners proclaim their villages, it is fun to try and work out where they come from by what they carry. It might be basketwork, or bowls of oranges, or ears of corn. Many of the girls carry baskets of cakes, bread and sweetmeats ostensibly to hand out to the crowd, though most of the recipients behave suspiciously like friends and relatives! An occasional guitar or accordion provides the accompaniment for cheerful folk songs as they pass.

After the traccas comes by far the largest contingent, the groups in costume, a dizzy, glittering colourful collection, many of the dresses hundreds of years old and so encrusted with jewels that they are kept in the bank vault in between occasions. The girls walk proudly, hands on hips, or delicately holding out the ends of their exquisite headscarves – until a friend calls from the crowd, when an animated conversation breaks out. Almost all the spectators are Sards, but they react to each costume group as if they have never seen it before.

The dresses are entirely suitable for cold winter wear, not quite so for a hot May day, because the long pleated skirts are made of orbace, a heavy woollen cloth which at one stage Fascist officers used for their uniforms. It is sheeps' wool, spun, dyed using local herbs, and woven by hand, and the permanent pleating, called a tabellas, is an ancient secret. The skirt reaches to the ankles and is invariably in a dark colour – blue, maroon, black, purple, brown, with one exception: mountain folk wear scarlet. On the rare occasions it is not pleated it is a heavy damask or brocade.

Over it is worn a shorter apron, often with a broad exotic silk border of embroidered flowers. The skirt and apron are the only common denominators in these costumes which subtly reveal marital status, wealth or otherwise, and sometimes livelihood, too. The three most distinctive items are the bodice or jacket, the headscarf or veil and the jewellery, all of which show how the dress was copied from the early Pisan or Aragonese domination of Sardinia; indeed some of them are almost perfect Elizabethan replicas, complete with ruff.

The girls from Assemini, for instance, wear a tight-fitting black velvet jacket with gold facings and a slit in the sleeve from elbow to wrist. Their lace bib is pure Spanish and a stiff collar stands up at the back, mediaeval-style. Ittiri has narrow purple velvet sleeves, while Atzara produces a gigantic puffed sleeve, as does San Vero Milis, which adds pleats to the ruff. Pirri's ruff is matched with a Spanish-style jacket; in the case of Buddoso the jacket is no more than a fringed bolero. These might all be described as lightweight and simple, compared to the other versions which put the girls into ornate padded bodices more like strait-jackets and sometimes with an over-jacket too.

A favourite feature is to have horizontal pleats running across the back of the bodice while adding all sorts of wondrous things such as embroidered flowers and lace to the front. Most of these corsets are tight-fitting and over them the jacket is added, not for extra warmth, which is quite unnecessary, but to hide the richness beneath. Siniscola girls cover their gold embroidered bodice with a scarlet jacket, the reason being that everyone in the village in the old days could afford the jacket, but not everyone the handsome under-garment, so you cover it up in order not to embarrass poorer neighbours.

Bachelors learn to recognise at a glance the unmarried girls. They will never have purely black aprons. Those from Aritzo wear a slender pink ribbon at their necks, to be changed to red when they marry. In Santadi the ribbon is scarlet for single and purple for married. And the wedding ring is the final give-away, an exquisite broad silver band with filigree embossed balls, and traditionally a present from the bridegroom's mother to the bride. The total effect so far is of an outfit that will quite easily stand on its own without anyone wearing it.

But there is yet more to be added, first the jewellery which, like the costumes, varies from the overdone to elegant sophistication – or, put more bluntly, knowing when to stop – a lesson well learned by Sarule which uses just two gold filigree buttons to join the top of the black bolero jacket with its outswept wings. Most of the costumes add a great deal more. Sometimes it is golden or silver chains across the bodice, like Iglesias; sometimes rings on every finger, each one attached to a golden chain linked to a golden waist belt like Quartu Sant'Elena; sometimes it is chokers and pendants and earrings set with gold, coral or silver; and in one dramatic style reflecting North African ancestry, from Villagrande, a silver chain stretches across the face. A final exotic touch, by Uri and Ittiri, are ten or a dozen silver or golden filigree balls that hang from the lower sleeve.

Nor is this the end of the richness. The final item is the head-dress where style reveals the historical background more sharply still. There are rare simple plain linen headscarves, like those of Bono, pinned under the chin; or in the case of Busachi a white linen square falling loose to the shoulders; or almost nun-like, starched and stiff as from Atzara; or striking blue and white silk from Iglesias. The other variations are anything but austere. Orgosolo's plain yellow headscarf turns out to be pure gold linen, and most villages are not content to leave it plain at all, and add not just silk embroidery in various colours, but overlay this with silver and gold thread and pearls. Cagliari has a scarlet felt mantilla with a border of silver embroidery. Other villages make the headscarf fringed, or of lace.

All are different and two, at least, are outstandingly distinctive. The first is that of Osilo, whose costume is plain black, with a double skirt at the back the top layer of which pulls up and over the head to form a cowl. It is, apparently, the most sombre costume of all, but when the cowl is allowed to fall back a magnificent padded head-dress is revealed in cream silk with embroidered flowers and inset panels of maroon velvet. The second is Desulo, one of the few that has discarded the headscarf in favour of a bonnet, Dutch-style, in bright orange, blue and gold, a most fetching affair, especially when worn with plaits neatly upended and pinned together across the top of the bonnet.

You might imagine that after this wealth of ornamentation in the women's dresses there would be very little left that the men could do to compete, and in a sense their costumes are much simpler and divide into two clear categories: those that reflect their way of life and those that are purely decorative, but the latter can amount to medieval court dress. Velvet scarlet, purple and blue jerkins are commonplace, fastened with silver or gold buttons, or, in the poorer villages, the jerkin made of felt and fastened with ribbons.

A man from Orgosolo is wearing his grandfather's costume, a splendidly Elizabethan affair with scarlet and blue velvet sleeves and an embroidered leather belt with a small pouch containing a faded Queen of Spades card which the old man, who died at the age of 102, kept for luck. The purpose of the pouch is variously described as a handy way to carry money – or cartridges! With the velvet jerkin goes an embroidered white linen blouse with voluminous sleeves and tight wrists, tied at the neck with silver buttons, black felt gaiters and to top the whole thing off, white pantalons worn under a short pleated black skirt of heavy wool. It can look like something out of Gilbert and Sullivan.

Alghero's costume is brand new, for they have not evolved one over the centuries of Spanish domination; they entered the festival for the first time in 1975, in eighteenth-century knee-length blue velvet trousers, slender velvet jacket with skinny scarlet tie, red cloth cummerbund and white linen shirt with Eton collar. Some purists may say this is cheating, but the costume is no less picturesque than those that have been handed down for generations.

The designs that reflect the livelihood of the wearers are much more realistic, practical and prosaic. The shepherds of Mogoro carry double shoulder bags, neatly embroidered, in which they place the cheese, wine and wafer-bread for their nomadic wanderings. They also carry a garment literally translated as a 'sack to cover', which is two lengths of heavy wool sewn together and can be used as a poncho, mackintosh or blanket. Tonara, a mountain hunting village, has a sheepskin jerkin called mastrucca, which comes down almost to the knees and is worn furry side inside during the winter.

Cabras, a fishing village, goes barefoot, the men simply clad in white shorts and a short skirt, scarlet for the engaged or courting, and black for the married, and lest the hint about what they do for a living is insufficient they carry fishing nets and lobster pots and a fish speared on a Neptune's trident. All those villages that weave – Elmas, Dorgali, Bitti, Collinas – have woven themselves a carpet banner to precede their processions. Sanluri makes bread and carries a very large round loaf in a circular basket. The shepherd villages do not bother with a banner but announce their arrival with a live young lamb carried on their shoulders. Desulo farmers wear the leather harness with which they carry their farm implements.

There is one final costume touch for the men, the famous black stocking cap called berritta, and how it is worn reveals all! When the tail is hanging down the wearer is engaged; when it is rolled up over the top of the cap the wearer is married. But in the Nuorese village of Baronia the tail of the cap hanging down to the left is said to reveal an outlaw! A couple of 'rebel' groups on the island refuse to conform to this tradition: San Pietro wears a Genoese cap, and Teulada goes Spanish with a pearly grey sombrero.

When the vast numbers of costume groups have finally sauntered past, there are three sets of riders. The first are the horsemen from the Campidano plain, whose mounts have be-ribboned tails and paper flowers stretching along their backs and across their foreheads. The riders wear black felt leggings, voluminous white trousers under short black skirts, a lace blouse with full sleeves and a brocade waistcoat. Their wives or girl friends ride side-saddle behind. They are followed by the Miliziani mounted troop, who have a North African look about them with their orange tunics, fez hats and swords. All the riders appear to have been born in the saddle and half-amuse, half-frighten the city spectators with their antics.

They are a cheerful merry contrast to the final set of horsemen, the dignified Alter Nos, representatives of the city and its craftsmen, originally members of mediaeval guilds. They ride slowly, in formal evening clothes, with white gloves, blue sashes, gold chain insignias and black top hats. Their sobering effect is deliberate, for behind them comes the mayor and a quartet of mace bearers preceding Sant'Efisio himself, a somewhat garish idol in

golden rococo cage carried on an oxencart and surrounded by choir boys and priests carrying delicate
golden lanterns. He is greeted with reverence, and more
than one spectator credits him with that day's warm
weather.

It has taken two hours for the parade to pass and
there is time only for a short rest and refreshment before
joining the admittedly smaller crowd who follow the Saint
on his two-day 25-mile journey by ox-cart to Nora, where
the original Efisio was martyred. This annual pilgrimage
is a grand excuse for a picnic by the seaside or in the
eucalyptus groves that line the shore, and to travel ten or
12 miles along the route on this day will take an hour or
more. The Saint makes his overnight stop at Sarroch,
with its hideous backcloth of oil refineries, but before that
there is a traditional pause at Villa d'Orri, a magnificent
private country house once occupied by the King of
Sardinia.

The ringing of the bells in the family chapel announces
his arrival, a romantic, almost bizarre sight as the oxen
plod up the tree-lined avenue to the courtyard. The
Saint's golden cage is piled high with fresh flowers and
thoughtfully provided with electric light so that he has a
brilliant entrance, preceded by mounted police who have
now changed into ordinary uniforms. There is enthusiastic
applause from the waiting crowd, who reach out to touch
Efisio's robes as he is carried into the chapel.

During the short service the oxen, who have been with
him all day and will take him on to Nora and back to
Cagliari three days hence, have their supper. A pile of
new grass is thrown down and their owner pushes it
gently into position so that they can eat well while still
yoked together. It is a short meal, for the Saint emerges,
is locked back in his golden cage and clatters off to
Sarroch. Those spectators who have fully participated in
the Sagra di Sant'Efisio have been on their feet for
approximately 14 hours.

There is, luckily, a few days' pause before Sardinia's
population descends upon its second largest town, Sassari,
in the north, for an equally important festival, the
Cavalcata Sarda. This started a couple of hundred years

ago as homage by the people to the Spanish kings, and is now a folklore event without religious overtones, but with extra additions such as famous inter-village horse racing and an evening, or rather night, of dancing. In the absence of a Saint to get things going, it was the Rotarians from Italy who reactivated the Cavalcata in its present form about 25 years ago, and since then it has been embellished and expanded to today's something-for-everyone holiday.

The same groups that appeared at Cagliari are once more brought in by bus, some of them leaving in the early hours, and each person receives a nominal 75 pence expenses. Two schools are turned over as dressing rooms and the buses disgorge modern teenagers whose long hair is eminently suitable for the costumes they are about to don. They are accompanied by various relatives in the way of dressers, and children to form the junior sections. It can be rightly described, at 7.30 a.m., as a mad-house, though among the confusion a stern order is eventually discernible. Each village has a classroom with its name upon the door, and that door is firmly closed against all comers while the dressing goes on.

Those who are ready begin to gather in the corridors, which are soon crammed with a seething mob. Wine and wafer-bread are passed around by the participants and there are small knots of serious people practising their singing or dancing. The sound of accordions and the mounting excitement gets at everyone. A father goes through complicated steps with his nine year old son; a very old man suddenly breaks into a solo dance; indeed song-and-dance is breaking out all over and even those in ordinary clothes cannot resist a jig.

It is fortunate that internal spirits are so high, for the weather is grey and spitting with rain. Rain is a hazard with which the organizers have never contended, and it is a serious matter, because those encrusted costumes can cost up to half a million pounds each. There is no way they can be exposed to bad weather and, worse, the end of the procession is at the Ippodromo Stadium, the local race course, and is preceded by horsemen who will churn the damp ground into mud, making the prospect of trailing the dresses through it a dismal one. The 9 a.m. start is postponed, but those who have seats in the stadium are urged to get there, for assuredly the Cavalcata will begin as soon as the rain stops.

The journey, in a heavy downpour, provides a classic example of the Sard character. The driver cannot believe that with his official sticker he is not allowed to go exactly where he pleases. The police are equally adamant that this street is closed. The law wins the altercation by directing us to the entrance that is nearest to the stands! The crowd is not as large as usual, on account of the weather, and out in the open, by the rails, the police stand forlornly in their raincoats with anorak hoods, with no-one to keep back but themselves.

Part of the parade does seem to be entering the stadium, though not in the right order. The gremi, members of the mediaeval guilds, the banner-carriers and mace bearers in scarlet uniforms trudge as far as the VIP platform when there is a sinister clap of thunder, a concerted groan and a new downpour. They and the visiting Scottish dancing team can be seen heading for cover. The announcer chats gamely on in Sard, French and English, but is drowned by the thunder. Even those in the covered stands raise their umbrellas against the rain blowing in at the sides. Rumour has it that the procession itself has been cancelled, but that the groups have been brought to the stadium in their buses so that at least the culmination of the event can take place.

Sadly, it is not to be, and at mid-day, almost in tears, the announcer tells the damp crowd that this year, for the first time ever, the Cavalcata is 'annulled'. Even the word has a despairing sound to it. But, should the rain clear, the palio, that is the inter-village horse races, will take place that afternoon as planned. The horses have been brought in by trailer and the main contest is expected to be, as usual, between Sedilo and Paulilatino. Whether or not the riders will be in a fit state to race seems to the outsider a little dubious. But the guide insists that these handsome fellows on their half-Arab horses drink brandy as a matter of course for breakfast, so the fact that they are cantering through the back

streets swigging red wine means nothing. Alas, the rain does not stop and the palio, too, is cancelled, and this in a year when the number of horses reaches 250, the highest ever.

There is still the evening programme and if it comes to the worst, arrangements are made for a few of the dancing groups to perform in a local gymnasium. No-one believes their Cavalcata can be reduced to this and the crowd hangs around, as usual, in Sassari's Piazza d'Italia. It does stop raining, the dancing begins exactly on time at 7 p.m. and makes up for everything. The official programme is discarded because those groups who have farthest to go have already been sent home, and it is a question of fitting in the remaining ones in an impromptu order depending upon who is ready and, understandably, who is capable. It has, after all, been a very long and bitter day of frustration for participants and spectators alike, and they have been flooding the cafes to drown their sorrows.

Quite the most cheery moment is the entry of the mamuthones into the Piazza, a grotesque sight accompanied by an equally grotesque noise. The group comes from Mamoiada, a mountain village renowned for banditry where only a few years ago a dozen members of one family were murdered in a vendetta. They represent hunted animals and are clad in shaggy black sheepskin jerkins hanging below their knees with a load of cowbells on their backs, the latter making the din. Black wooden masks are carried in front of their faces and they top off the ensemble with a purple scarf over their stocking caps, for all the world like cartoon characters suffering from toothache! What with their costumes and the racket and their total disregard for the order of performance, they certainly bring an outlaw touch to the proceedings.

The stage is quickly cleared, and they lumber on, accompanied by their partners the issokadores, representing the hunters. These fellows wear a scarlet linen jacket, a fringed scarf tied around the waist and carry lassos with which they 'capture' selected members of the audience. This leads to quite a tangle as the lasso has a knot on the end, making it an unwieldy object to retrieve as it snakes back to the stage catching shoulders, arms and handbags on the way. The dance, if it can be so called, is meanwhile going on, with the dozen mamuthones in slow-motion crossing the platform in a shambling walk with occasional small jumps. They could hardly do more, encumbered by 28lbs of bells apiece, and they finish their act in their own good time, ignoring the instructions on the programme that no group shall perform for more than ten minutes.

The dancing proper is a much more delicate affair, only marginally hampered by the earlier rain which has reduced the stage surface to that of a wavy beach. It is not only costume detail that reveals marital status; so do the dances. The young man with a girl on each arm is a bachelor. But custom does not permit him to hold the girls' hands. He has a handkerchief in each hand and his partners hold the other end of it. The fellow with only one partner is either married or courting.

Unlike the parade groups, the dancers carry no identification, but there is no mistaking some of them. Cabras, for instance, the fishing village, remains barefoot as it has done all day, and its dance is a simple one, almost a walking step with the knees bent, accompanied by a launeddas pipe-player with a sound not unlike bagpipes but more reedy. It is particularly apt that Cabras should use this ancient Sard instrument, for the special reeds of which it is made are found in the marshes in their neighbourhood. The pipe is actually a three-in-one affair. The basso, the largest and thickest, is about a yard long and the other two shorter pipes provide the upper registers. Most of the music this evening is provided by either pipes, guitar or accordion.

Some dances have a pastoral boy-meets-girl flavour, others symbolize fire worship with the dancers closing up in a tight circle and moving very fast. A particular one crops up again and again and is called Ballu Tundu, the round dance. Its repetitive quality reflects the monotonous life of the sheperds who dance it and sometimes, like Sarule's version, it sounds Slavonic. Almost every group produces its own soloists, pairs who step out of the swaying line to swirl madly round and round and then fall back to be replaced by another pair. By now, one hour into the programme, there are 5000 spectators, balloon-sellers amongst them, and little knots in the crowd who cannot resist the hypnotic music and rhythm are forming their own dancing circles.

One of the organizers keeps up an informative running commentary for me on the finer points of the dances, including some cutting criticism. Alghero, taking part for the first time, are pooh-poohed as making it up as they go along. Sennori's team, too, is said to be non-authentic, though the organizer admits they dance quite well. Ollolai comes in for his warmest praise as well as his most devastating criticism. They dance beautifully, he says, and indeed they have been visible in a corner of the square practising for several hours before their performance. Unfortunately, he adds, they have the ugliest women on the island, and lest that sounds too harsh a judgment, he says that it is their high cheek bones that mar their beauty. They are led by a bricklayer and, high cheek bones or not, are one of the most popular turns of the night.

Also popular are any groups that include children, who are greeted with warm and affectionate applause irrespective of their expertise. The children take their roles most seriously and while they appear to be wearing a miniature version of the adult costume there are subtle differences and no girl is qualified for the full costume until she is 20 years of age. But however small the girls, they can do the graceful turn and swirl that precedes sitting down on the stage for a pause and ensures that the long pleated skirt falls in an elegant circle around them.

The poorer villages have never possessed musical instruments, so they have evolved a system of manipulating their voices to provide the equivalent. It is an extraordinary sound, but the drum and flute and the twang of a stringed instrument are clearly discernible. Orgosolo, not poor, is an expert at this, with a complete choir as the orchestra, plus a madrigal quartet who improvise the verses to the joy of the crowd. One number, quite unrecognisable to the foreigner, turns out to be Ave Maria in a Sard dialect.

This part of the Cavalcata lasts for six hours, disappointingly short by Sard standards, but it is a cold night and shortly after 1 a.m. the Piazza has emptied of both performers and spectators, relieved that their festival was not entirely annulled after all. It will be a short night's sleep if you want to attend the highlight of the third famous event, for without fail you must arrive in Nuoro Province by lunchtime the next day, to drive to Lula and the feast of San Francesco at the church of the same name.

The celebration, like a number of similar ones in Sardinia, runs for nine days, with one unique difference from the others: it was begun by, is organized by and continued by bandits who, several hundred years ago, promised they would build a church for St Francis if he in his turn ensured their continuing freedom. Each year, in early May, they gather here, living in little rooms around the church, for a part-social part-religious holiday, and there is a sort of immunity within the precincts. Local newspapers describing the event talk of the pilgrims leaving outside their everyday life (a euphemism for guns), and their passions (a euphemism for vendettas). The police visit – but there are no arrests on this neutral ground.

San Francesco church sits remotely in the green hilly countryside of this mountainous province and outside the gates the stallholders are selling nougat, cob nuts, peanuts and so on to arriving pilgrims who head first for a shabby workman's cafe, to be greeted with coffee and sponge fingers, symbolizing a welcome to travellers. The conversational level is exceedingly loud and when the cafe empties for the early afternoon lull the proprietor helpfully turns up the record player to top volume to replace the missing noise. Food is provided on a community basis and all the workers are pilgrims themselves, taking it in turns to do the chores.

Sardinia is famous for its wafer-bread and here is made a special kind, just for the festival. It is called Filindeu, has the appearance of fine straw matting and is broken into pieces to be dropped into a cheesey soup. Next on the menu is a platter of cold meats – joints and knuckles of lamb and chicken tossed in a pile – with side dishes of cold potatoes and olives, the whole eaten, mediaeval-style, with the fingers. This is followed by Sanguinaccio, the stomach of a sheep stuffed with nuts, sugar, lemon, mint, cheese and grated wafer-bread, eaten very hot and very filling. It could be a long-lost cousin of haggis, but it is more herby and bloody.

The meal ends with casu, a very hard sheep's milk cheese. The pilgrim cook, a giant of a man, is concerned that the visitor does not seem able to eat all of this lunch, and feeds me by hand, like a baby, even cutting off a piece of cheese and removing the rind before handing it over. In the meantime, the long trestle tables have been removed and the chairs placed around the walls in preparation for the expected flood of last-minute arrivals for the culminating event of the nine days. This consists of the service and ceremony at which this year's organizer of the feast hands over his reins of office to the next man, with the title of prior, though neither he nor his predecessor have anything to do with the clergy.

Before mass, however, there is afternoon visiting around the 50 or so little rooms like stables that are built with collection money on the perimeter of the church courtyard. Into each room is crammed a family and there is not a bit of untidiness anywhere. Shoes are put on the windowsill to keep them out of the way, and a curtain divides the beds from the living area, with flowers on the table. There is a miniature stove and gas light, but no running water.

The first family I visit, at random, comprises three sisters, the husband of one of them, and a great aunt who looks like a centenarian. Cakes and wine are served, and a box of macaroons pressed upon the visitor. The next room is occupied by the wife of one of the ex-priors and like most women here she is wearing the everyday national costume of chocolate-brown long pleated skirt. There is more wine, more cake, and a bag of sponge fingers to take away, and it is fortunate that the priest and altar-boys arrive before the tonnage of sweetmeats and the intake of liquor paralyses the visitor completely.

Everybody who can get into the church does so, the

overflow cramming the porch and vestry. The pulpit is full of small boys and the excellent choir turns out to be a local music school which is taking part in that year's Eisteddfod in Wales. It breaks into the Hallelujah Chorus from Handel's Messiah. The priest makes a friendly speech, hardly a sermon, and blesses both outgoing and incoming prior. Everybody claps, while those nearest rush to embrace the men and the choir sings a chant to St Francis.

No one quite knows how long this ceremony has been going on, but a wall plaque lists the years when it was not possible to hold the festival, the first of these being 1890. The post-church celebration is in the cafe, the informal procession of priest, altar-boys, priors, close friends and relatives 'played in' by fellow pilgrims beating the iron lids of enormous cooking pots. This inner sanctum ceremony is an emotional one. The amateur cymbalists stand on chairs the better to beat their lids, everyone kisses the new prior and his wife and the old prior and his wife, and everyone is in floods of tears, including a trio of carabinieri. When I try to leave gracefully I am just as gracefully put back in my chair and more macaroons and liqueurs are produced.

Outside in the courtyard at dusk the choir practices for its forthcoming trip to Wales, and very many pilgrims wander about carrying basket-covered wine jugs and pressing a glass upon anyone who will take it. Only the oldest of the old men, in brown corduroy suits and riding boots, sit quietly beneath the tamarisk trees. Those too young to drink amuse themselves with the game of murra, a sharp action of the fist springing open to reveal so many fingers, the winner being the one who not only guesses the number his opponent will produce, but moves his own fist the fastest.

The feasting and fun will clearly go on most of the night and the next day, the end of the festival, all the pilgrims return to Nuoro by car, horse or motor bike, bringing a statue of St Francis with them and pausing on the way for a mammoth picnic where lamb and pig are roasted over juniper-wood fires.

3 Cagliari

The Phoenicians took one look at Cagliari's safe anchorage and potential port facilities and decided it was for them. Their view was shared by everyone throughout history up to and including the Second World War when it was badly damaged by Allied bombing. Much that was precious, though, survived, and to it has been added all the twentieth-century bustle and vitality of a capital, with the assets of a life tuned to a Mediterranean climate. This latter makes it tailor-made for sightseeing: walking tours during the mornings, when the first discovery is that the city is built on several hills, followed by a drink at a comfortable pavement cafe in the Via Roma to watch the comings and goings at the port.

All activity then ceases until the rush-hour traffic floods back in shortly before 5 p.m. on a one-way system which is the despair of new arrivals. Luckily, legs are more important than a motor car for the first day or two, so to get a feel of the shape and size of Cagliari walk up the central hill to the district appropriately called Castello, for it is the old walled city, as intact as it has been for centuries, complete with ramparts and towers. The most spectacular approach is from Piazza Costituzione via a flight of steps to an elegant archway which conjures up a mansion on the other side instead of the St Remy Bastion. The steps were in fact added during the nineteenth century and the bastion turns out to be a two-level enormous piazza with palms and pine trees and seats, the higher level called Terrazza Umberto I and a favourite sunset spot.

From here, go down the steps on the other side of the

bastion to the old city and the University, which is the original eighteenth-century building designed by Captain Belgromo di Famolasco and is still in use, though with the increasing number of students much of the campus is now in the suburbs. Beyond it is the first of the two famous towers, the Tower of the Elephant, built in 1307 during Pisan domination by the Sard architect Giovanni Capula. Its name comes not from its shape but from a statue of the animal set on a high ledge. It is a massive mediaeval construction with, curiously, only three sides enclosed and the fourth towards the city left open so that its interior wooden struts give it a somewhat unfinished look. This is wholly deceptive because the tower and its brother at the opposite end of the ramparts were the two most important defensive points of the castle of Cagliari.

The capture had not been an easy victory for the Pisans, who first had to beat the Saracens and then the Genoese. The latter, in fact, were in possession of the castle for a while but relinquished it when they received Sassari as compensation. Once it was back in their hands, the Pisans set about adding to the fortifications, a wise precaution because they were about to be invaded in 1323 by the Infante Don Alfonso, son of the Aragonese King. His Admiral arrived in Cagliari harbour with a substantial fleet and disembarked more than 10,000 troops.

Meanwhile Don Alfonso, who had captured Iglesias, was marching to meet him. The strength of the enemy was too much for the Pisans. They made an unsuccessful attempt to kidnap Alfonso's wife, Dona Teresa, then capitulated. The Aragonese allowed them to stay on, but held them as feudal subjects and demanded annual tributes. The new conquerors were around for the next 400 years but they left the fortifications just as they were – and just as you see them now.

From the Tower of the Elephant any street going upwards will do, past old houses, some with crests above the doorways indicating their original merchant ownership, but largely crumbling and unpainted. Those without fine stone doorways have a simple stable door so that the inhabitants can lean companionably out ignoring the television blaring within. The narrow streets also mean that householders on opposite sides can chat quietly to each other at ground level, or from the balconies on the first, second, third or even fourth floors. Sooner or later, probably by Via La Marmora, you will arrive in Piazza Palazzo, which is two-level, the lower one being an attractive row of town houses and the upper level containing a quartet of important buildings.

Dominating the Piazza is the cathedral of San Cecilia described by D. H Lawrence in 'Sea and Sardinia' thus: 'It must have been a fine old pagan stone fortress once. Now it has come, as it were, through the mincing machine of the ages, and oozed out baroque and sausagey.' The church was originally built between 1257 and 1312 in romanesque style and got its baroque interior from Domenico Spotorno in the seventeenth century. This was changed once more, quite recently, in 1933, by the architect Giarrizzo who added neo-Pisan touches. The facade, with four sets of arches set at different levels, is now a mellow yellow with a grey thirteenth-century bell-tower.

There are three carved wooden doors and as soon as you have entered, turn your back on the altar so that you face the door you have just come in to see two magnificent stone pulpits, originally part of a single pulpit made in 1159-1162 by Maestro Guglielmo for the cathedral of Pisa. They were given as a present to Cagliari in 1312 when Giovanni Pisano sculpted another pulpit for Pisa. The quartet of lions that have stood guard at the foot of the altar steps since the seventeenth century were also a part of the original pulpit.

The cathedral, as you would expect with its history, is very ornate, with rounded arches and square pillars separating the three naves, and a floor of black, white and mottled pink marble. The gems to be seen in the main body of the church include: in one of the baroque side chapels, a fourteenth-century gold-painted wooden madonna and child with charming natural faces; a silver tabernacle on the altar dating from 1610 and looking sadly tarnished; and the mausoleum of Martin II of Aragon, who died in 1409, by the seventeenth-century Geonese sculptor Giulio Aprile. It is in the same mottled marble as the floor, with life-size angels and warriors fronted by a simple tomb.

While the presbytery is a small room reached by four steps, it has no less than five doors in addition to the fifteenth-century Aragonese-gothic cross-vaulted ceiling from which is suspended a silver lamp made in 1602 by Giovanni Mameli. One door leads into the Aula Capitolare with a collection of paintings, among which is a scourging of Christ attributed to Guido Reni. From here you can reach the Museo Capitolare housing the treasures, but on this day the door is locked. I am told that it contains a fifteenth-century gold and silver cross carried around Cagliari in the Feast of Corpus Christi procession, a silver plate and goblet said to be the work of Benvenuto Cellini, and a triptych by the Flemish painter Gerard David. Legend has it that the latter was stolen by a Spanish mercenary from the bedside of Pope Clement VII during the sacking of Rome, and that the thief gave it to Cagliari cathedral in repentance and gratitude for being saved in a shipwreck near Sardinia's capital when he was on his way home with the stolen loot.

By far the most stunning and unusual part of the cathedral is the Sanctuary reached through a door on the altar steps to bring you into the central one of three chapels at almost ceiling level, with a chance to see closely the carved motives and flowers that cover it, before going down the flight of steps to subterranean level. This part of the Sanctuary is dedicated to the seventeenth-century Bishop Esquivel who built it 300 years after the foundation of the cathedral itself. A second chapel is the mausoleum, sculpted by Andrea Galassi, of Marie Josephine Louise, wife of Louis XVIII of France. She died in exile in 1810 at Hartwell in Buckinghamshire, and it was at her own request – as the daughter of Vittorio Amadeo II, King of Sardinia – that her body was brought to Cagliari a year after her death. The third chapel has the tomb of Carlo Emanuele of Savoy, the infant son of Vittorio Emanuele I and Maria-Theresa of Austria, who died in 1799.

Perhaps the most interesting aspect of the Sanctuary,

however, is not these tombs, but the walls, which are hewn out of rock and into which were carved by seventeenth-century Sicilian artists a vast array of niches with bas-reliefs of all the Sardinian Saints. Their ashes were said to have been found beneath the ruins of the church of San Saturnino in 1617 and, as Tyndale puts it: 'The number of these martyrs is so appalling, that if one has any faith in the identity of their remains, Cagliari must have been a species of religious slaughter-house.'

The cathedral is flanked by two imposing buildings. One is the Governor's Palace, built in 1769 by Davisto, which was formerly the royal palace of the House of Savoy and contains valuble frescoes by Domenico Bruschi as well as large ornate rooms. The other is the even larger and more imposing Archbishop's Palace, by the same architect. The seventeenth-century Music Conservatory on the opposite corner completes the quartet in the Piazza Palazzo. A short walk from here up Via Martini brings you to one end of the walled city and to Piazza Indipendenza where stands the brother tower to that of the Elephant, this one called San Pancrazio, with the same curious open side which you can climb up for the view.

In one corner of the Piazza stands the National Archaeological Museum looking from the outside like a gracious private house with a fine tree covering half its façade. Above it is an art gallery showing the development of painting in Sardinia from the fourteenth to the seventeenth centuries and a second gallery, the municipal one, at the end of the public gardens in Viale S. Vincenzo, continues this history of painting and includes various sculptures. But, to be honest, it is not pictures you come to see here, but the finest collection of nuraghic objects.

The nucleus of the museum was the private collection of Carlo Felice who in 1806 gave it to the University, since when it has been greatly expanded. Of the nuraghic items, the most spectacular are contained in several show-cases, the famous bronze statuettes varying in height from four inches to about a foot and a half. Historians differ as to where the Proto-Sards got their inspiration for the designs; but the subject matter was certainly no problem. They merely looked about them and depicted their way of life. As they left no writing this art is one of the main keys to these ancient people.

It is also unique in that you do not need to be an historian or an archaeologist to appreciate it. I find that my notes ramble on and on with descriptions of the contents of the three or four cases which range down the middle of a fairly small room. There is no catalogue or literature, but the bronzes speak for themselves and subdivide neatly into three main areas of interest: the human figures representing deities, chiefs and the jobs and pastimes of the people; the votive boats; and the domestic items in the way of chests, lamps and so on.

The gods are about equally divided between male and female, the women making offerings or holding babies quite out of proportion to the mother's size. In one of the larger bronzes a female surrealistic figure with pronounced breasts has square flaps for arms making her into a shape like a cross. The male figures tend to strike dramatic poses, especially if they are chiefs or warriors, in which case they are hung about with weapons in the way of sticks, daggers, spears, swords, shields, and sometimes dressed in a primitive mail-chain suit with horned headgear. Some are decidedly modernistic, having four eyes and four arms, or half bull and half man, while the others are precise representations.

Those statuettes depicting craftsmen and sportsmen have a marvellous vitality about them. They include a man carrying a gourd, a fellow with a rough lasso, a shepherd, a hunter with an animal across his shoulders, a rider on a bull, a couple of wrestlers, one kneeling upon the other, and a whole series of archers with bows as high as themselves. Some are merely carrying them, others are shooting, and one is standing on the back of an unidentifiable animal. The animals themselves are fascinating, because the individual character comes through and it would be easy to differentiate between bull and cow even if the former had no horns; an arrogant raised head, a nose lowered to sniff, ears perked up, all help to give the mood. Again, some are purely representational, like a running fox and a fierce wild boar, while others have two heads and no legs, or are in the form of Siamese twins.

Most stylish of all are the votive boats. Their bowsprits have figureheads of horned animals, sometimes with a bird perched between the horns, and the sides of each craft have delicate upraised railings on which are sitting birds and animals. Sometimes the birds replace the row-locks. Whatever the design, the whole effect is totally charming. The domestic side of nuraghic life is, naturally, more prosaic, and shows bowls and oil-holders from the eighth-century B.C., and two-handled jugs, the items becoming more sophisticated the newer they are. There is, for instance, a miniature chest with handles and four legs which would not be out of place today, and an ornate lamp in the shape of a fine boat.

It is very probable that after this Proto-Sard feast you will have had enough for one day and prefer to come again – the entrance is free – to take in the rest of the museum. Certainly you need a break for the next exhibits are centuries later in Punic-Roman with a change in both scale and material. The statues are life-size with Romans in togas or warrior dress. The terracotta busts depict muses and gods and were mostly found locally; the funeral urns are fine stone carved sarcophagi depicting, variously, cherubs, centaurs, nymphs and so on; and there is a very large mosaic patterned with squares and circles.

Other important finds from this age come from Thar-ros, a ruined Roman town, which exhibits funeral stones, coffins, tombs with paintings, a sinister sacrificial altar and a sacred lion. Perhaps the most interesting of this section to a non-expert is a series of strange figures from Bithia, another old settlement, all representing the God Bes who got up to all sorts of antics including arranging marriages. He is depicted with an enormous Simple Simon head, a great round body ending at the waist and very long arms.

The display of Roman jewellery is substantial and inc-ludes a couple of engraved gold panels no bigger than postcards, one with writing found at Nora and the other a frieze of human figures with animal heads. The glass-ware, mostly from Tharros, Karalis (the Roman name for Cagliari) and Cornus, is in the form of vases, with or without handles, and the final room is an extensive coin collection from Punic, Roman, Byzantine, Arab and Spanish times.

Outside the museum in Piazza Indipendenza there is an easy exit from the old city via a one-car archway which is the old entry to the city. This leads into Piazza Arsenale which has no less than three one-way archways, one of which will take you into Viale Regina Elena flank-ed by the thick fortress walls on one side and a broad terrace and garden on the other. Walk down the hill and you will be back in Piazza Costituzione.

Leaving the walled city as a motorist can be a rather extra-ordinary experience, for there seems to be only one driv-able road that actually enables you to get the other side of the walls. All the others end abruptly, either with bol-lards or, more disconcertingly, with a flight of steps. At one point I thought I would have to abandon the car on a staircase, which is nothing like as crazy as it sounds, since several cars are nonchalantly parked on some of the shallower flights. Finally, after innumerable false trails, the road out is found, leading down the hill from the Castello quarter of Cagliari.

These fortifications are by no means the only surviving ancient part, indeed the next period of history to be investigated is even older, that of the Romans who made Cagliari the most important commercial centre in the south of the island. Although they were not actually opposed by the Sards, they had the Vandals and Goths on their tails whose commanders had resounding names but whose conquests were relatively short-lived. The Romans were firmly established by the mid-sixth century A.D. and held on for the duration of their Empire, to be succeeded, briefly, by the Saracens.

Despite the problems of warding off other would-be conquerors, the Romans found time for development and building and they left behind some substantial slabs of architecture, albeit rather scattered. They were involved in, though they did not build, the oldest and most important Christian monument in Sardinia, the basilica of San Saturnino, in Piazza S. Cosimo, also known as the church of Santi Cosimo e Damiano, standing on the spot where Saturnus was martyred during the reign of the Roman Emperor Diocletian. The original unfinished, part-pagan fifth-century construction became the nucleus of an early sixth-century church whose foundations were used by the monks of Saint-Victor at Marseilles for the church they built in 1089-1119.

The basilica is a little distance from the city centre in a busy residential district and has been given lots of breathing space in the way of a walled garden where excavations are still taking place. How to find the key to the garden gate is one of those problems that the keen sightseer in Sardinia soon learns to solve. Drop in for a cup of coffee at the cafe in the Piazza and the propriet-ress will willingly give explicit instructions. Walk along the Via S. Lucifero which runs along one side of the square, and go up the steps into the modern church of San Lucifero where mass is about to start in one of the side chapels. Creep past to the door marked Parochial Office from which there are faint sounds of a typewriter and inside is a fellow who just by the appearance of the visitor knows the requirements. He hands over two keys, with a request that they be returned.

Back in the Piazza, the first key opens the padlock on the outer iron gate into the garden forecourt and the second, after six turns, the main door. The basilica itself is exquisite, despite the damage it received from bombing on May 13, 1943. A panel inside depicts the result of that bombardment, including how the thick walls with-stood the blast, and the progress of the reconstruction with the original stones from September 1943, to May 1952. It is in the form of a Greek cross, two arms of which are eleventh century, and at the back in the dome section, are four Roman pillars set into wall niches, which are pink in colour, two of them with friezes.

Four out of the six columns in the nave survived, with delicate fluted vertical lines down them and a frieze of figures around the top. the two reconstructed columns have an original base and top. Everything is rounded,

anticipating romanesque. There are two fore-shorten-
ed side naves, in both of which there are signs of excavations to reach the original pagan-Christian necropolis.
There is no pulpit and no proper altar, just a table with
a white cloth upon it, a microphone and a surplice
thrown casually across.

Outside in the courtyard beneath tall palm trees, a
quartet of cannon balls is embedded in the ground, and
there are Roman sarcophagi and various bits of old stone
with Latin inscriptions. Unfortunately there is no way of
getting a close view of the ancient necropolis in the surrounding garden because all but the area which gives
access to the basilica has been blocked off. You can, however, peer through the iron bars set into the wall to see
that the exterior excavations, including a pagan temple,
join up with those inside the church.

Another piece of Roman architecture of a very different
kind is the home of Tigellius, a Sardinian poet and
singer. He was much favoured by the Roman Emperor
Augustus as well as by Caius Caesar and Cleopatra,
which could have been one reason why Horace and
Cicero loathed him and missed no chance to ridicule his
work. Cicero, indeed, once referred to Tigellius as 'a man
more pestilential than his country', the other pestilence
being malaria. The poet's house, in Via Tigellio, or what
remains of it, is quite large and stands on the corner of a
modern residential area with blocks of flats. There are
two columns of the portico and several pieces of wall up
to waist-height dotted about among the poppies and
grass.

A bus ride distant, squashed between the houses on the
busy main Viale S. Avendrace, is the Grotto of the Viper,
the tomb of an exiled Roman pair and so called because
above the portal are sculpted two serpents wriggling towards each other. There had been a suggestion that a
call at the local police station might produce the
whereabouts of the custodian, but on a hot afternoon the
journey seemed too much of an effort, and, anyway, most
of the tomb can be seen through the barred gate while
standing on the pavement.

The construction, dug out of limestone, is as high as a

three-storey house and in its forecourt are a couple of shrubs and a lot of uncut grass. To the right of the main tomb is a small sarcophagus and a semi-circular row of niches that could have held ashes. The inscriptions are too far away to read, but in any case they are in Latin and Greek and dedicated to Atilia Pomptilla by her husband, Cassius Philippus, two high-born Romans who were exiled here. It seems that when Cassius, who had been married to Atilia for 42 years, was about to die, his devoted wife offered her own life to save his and shortly afterwards went off into a sleep from which she never awoke. On Cassius's death he was buried in the same place.

To the side of the tomb a flight of steps leads up past dilapidated houses to the Punic necropolis on the top of the hill that was the cemetery of ancient Karalis. The area has been fenced off, but nothing else has been done and the custodian's house but not, alas, the custodian, can be seen in front of the row of holes in the rock face that mark the entrances to the tombs. At least one tomb, outside the fencing, appears to have been converted into an annexe for a nearby house, with a canopy of corrugated iron over its entrance and a gourd hanging up outside.

Geographically, it is convenient to continue along the Viale S. Avendrace to the Catello San Michele, although it means leaving the Romans momentarily. This fortress right on the outskirts of town is reached with difficulty from Viale Monastir through a modern housing estate as I discovered when I visited it. At the top of a steep winding narrow road you suddenly come to a Zone Militare notice and around the next bend is a barred gate behind which are a couple of sailors and an Alsatian guard dog. Clearly it is not open to the public, but the thought of reversing down the hairpin bends seemed so appalling that I asked the sailors if I could just drive through the gate and turn round in the flat space beyond. I expressed a wistful interest in the castle and with beaming smiles the gates were opened, not just to allow me to reverse, but to show me the historic fortifications.

The 24-year-old sailor who had learnt English at school, proved an excellent guide and we took a detour to avoid going anywhere near the radio station they were guarding. San Michele was built in 1216 as a Carthusian monastery then called Bonvei, and was converted into a fortress by the Pisans on their possession of Cagliari. During the wars between the Pisans and the Aragonese, the latter added their own defences and it finally became the personal property of a Spanish family. When they retired to Spain it lapsed for several years before being turned into a military hospital. Now the castle is a forlorn, derelict construction standing between radio masts.

On this tour, with the best views of Cagliari, sea and surrounding countryside, we were accompanied by a playful three-month-old puppy. The moat, now overgrown, has a walled channel running away from it and the sailor told me that if, when attacking, the enemy seemed in danger of taking the castle, the inmates would have retaliated by opening the floodgates and drowning them. It also contains a fresh water well, still obviously functioning because around it are a cluster of flourishing wild fig trees. The entrance to the castle has been half-bricked up, but this did not deter my guide who climbed nimbly up and helped me into the courtyard, where the difference in architectural styles between the one Aragones tower and the remaining Pisan tower is pronounced. While all the intervening floors have disappeared, the towers still have arrow-slits and emplacements for cannon. The dungeons, now open to the sky, fail to look as sinister as the enclosed guardhouse. We finally clambered out, covered in chalk, to be greeted ecstatically by the puppy.

Back in the centre of the city there remains one more important heritage from Roman times, the Amphitheatre. It should be a landmark easy to find, but in fact trying to reach it by car produces an unexpected problem, because when it is below the level of the road you cannot see it. The best plan is to park somewhere in Viale Fra Ignazio da Laconi and stroll from there. The Amphitheatre was built about the same time as the Coliseum in Rome, was almost completely carved out of rock and is in a very good state of repair.

There is a semi-circle of tamarisks at the top of the hill, and the tiered stone seats slope downwards with occasional cypresses scattered below and bounded by the lush greenery of the Botanical Gardens beyond. The modern flats that have grown up on one side do not intrude too much. From the roadside you can see the dungeons where wild beasts were kept, and in an endeavour to get the keys to the bolted gates I landed up in an old people's home which turned out to be run by the Capucines. They did not have the keys, but they had something else to show me, their church in Viale Fra Ignazio da Laconi, after which the street is named.

Ignatius is yet another Saint particularly beloved by the Cagliarese. His ashes are in the Capucine church and there is a small bare cell where he lived, through whose bars presents have been pushed, while the wall outside is plastered with pictures of grateful recipients of his healing powers. Almost opposite are the Botanical Gardens, which in the mornings are the leafy green refuge of mothers and children who gather around the fountain and lily pond. The perambulators are 'dressed' for summer with basket-work chassis and gingham frills and canopy.

Down the hill from the gardens is the medical complex with hospital, clinic and students, and from Viale Fra Ignazio you will come to the church of San Michele with its seventeenth-century handsome baroque façade. There are three archways leading into the porch and if you walk straight on absent-mindedly, you will end up at the military hospital. Turn right to get into the church, passing a fine stone pulpit in the porch. The interior is very ornate, with marble altars in tones of white, black, brown and red. A statue of St Michael looks half warrior, with his tunic, and half angel, with his golden wings.

The best view of the façade is from Via Azuni, a narrow and interesting street, passing the church of Sant'Anna with its two towers and nineteenth-century façade and bringing you into Piazza Yenne where stalls are set up beneath the palm trees. This mini-market specializes in cheap clothes and trinkets and political slogans painted on cardboard exhort the shoppers: 'There are millions on our backs and this is the only law the Neapolitan bosses know; learn to assassinate them.' The violent anti-Italian sentiments are being universally ignored.

From the Piazza the wide boulevard, Largo Carlo Felice, leads down to the waterfront and Piazza Matteotti, with the gothic monstrosity of the twin-towered Palazzo Comunale, originally built in the nineteenth century by Crescentino Caselli It was partly destroyed during the Second World War and rebuilt exactly as before. Inside, however, there are a couple of treasures: paintings by Filippo Figari and a triptych by the sixteenth-century Cagliarese artist, Pietro Cavaro. Stretching away from the Piazza is the Via Roma, a long colonnaded pavement with cafés and shops and the place for the evening promenade.

A group of American, Moroccan and German hippies have set up their wares, and sailors are among the passing throng. The street is actually two two-way streets with palm trees in the middle, so you need to shout above the 'quadruple' rush-hour traffic. By 8 p.m. the crowd is diminishing and the hippies pack up, but only for a couple of hours until the after-dinner crowd emerges. At the back of the Via Roma is a maze of narrow streets and some of the best restaurants in Cagliari, in Via Sardegna.

First, however, to find a parking place for the hired car. In order to offload the luggage at the hotel here I have been obliged to hold up all the traffic behind me as the street, already lined with cars on one side, cannot permit them to pass. The Cagliarese understand the problem and wait patiently. What then to do with the car is neatly solved by the hotel manager who sends a bell-boy to run in front and find a space. With fine disregard for the Highway Code or any traffic laws, the lad turns sharp left into a no-entry street and beckons me firmly to follow to the miniscule parking space he has found. Guiltily, I ditch the car, ostentatiously facing the wrong way, and hope for the best.

Via Sardegna has none of the bustle of the waterfront Via Roma, but the restaurants are those used by the locals and I pick one at random, obviously a popular choice as there is no table available. Both the proprietor and a waiting young couple are desperately anxious that I should not misconstrue the situation and leave. A few minutes later a place is free and everyone smiles in relief that the stranger is settled.

The kitchen is in splendid view, with a flurry of people stirring enormous pans into one of which is tossed a live lobster. I order salsiccia, a local smoked sausage which turns out to be rich, piquant and filling, with a bean salad. The other diners include a table of ten men and a quartet of old characters one of whom, in moments of extreme conversational excitement, removes his cloth cap, to replace it when the talk simmers down. There are murmurs of approval from all of us when the proprietor passes by carrying a gigantic bass.

If you want to eat out of the city, the beach area at Poetto is nearby with its own little harbour and a long promenade lined with restaurants and terrace cafés, and most of the sand is covered in beach huts. This is the place to avoid at weekends, but an alternative – and you still get the sea breeze – is to drive over the Stagno di Santa Gilla on the Pula road. While there is no sandy playground for quite a long way there is a simple restaurant which will provide a memorable meal.

Drive slowly, because all you see from the road is a cluster of shabby little houses, one of which is painted pink and has a faded sign. It looks no more than a good pull-up for lorry drivers and nothing inside dispels this impression until you hopefully mention lobsters, when the young patron forcibly seizes you and drags you into the kitchen to select your own. My meal was augmented, with unfailing Sard hospitality, by five men at the next table who had a gigantic platter of red mullet which they were demolishing with their fingers. A sample was sent over for the foreigner to try and her offer to return something in the way of a bottle of wine smilingly refused. Both mullet and lobster were delicious, which satisfied the patron, the local customers and the visitor.

It is just the ample nourishment required to set off on a final tour of Cagliari. Because of World War II destruction you would expect to find large sections of modern buildings, and indeed they are visible, but the finest examples of twentieth-century work can be seen in three quite different churches. The church of the Carmine, in Viale Trieste, was originally built in 1580 and completely destroyed in 1943. Ghino Venturi designed the post-war replacement in an understated modern style, with pillars of grey and cream horizontal stripes and a vast mural behind the altar. The street leads into Piazza del Carmine which has lots of trees and benches, an exceedingly ugly statue in its centre and a little market at one end.

The church of San Domenico, in Via San Domenico, presents another puzzle on how to gain entry. When I visited everything was locked and I was directed to the seminary and school next door and seated in what looked like a private hallway while the maid went off in search of someone. A priest emerged who spoke a little English, bringing with him a man with a bunch of keys who accompanied me. We began with the crypt, the only part of the Aragonese-gothic church that withstood war damage. The custodian would have done well at the Royal Academy of Dramatic Art with his graphic histrionics of the destruction.

What has survived at this level is a beautiful romanesque stone archway with a carved flower motif, a plain stone altar and some of the columns. One aisle of the sixteenth-century cloisters with its elegant cross-vaults is completely untouched; the rest is in pieces lying about waiting to be re-positioned. It can be disconcerting to find the tranquillity suddenly broken by a boisterous collection of seminary school-boys who use the cloisters as their playground.

Built above the crypt is the modern post-war church, designed by Raffaele Fagnoni. The bell-tower stands separately on the broad flight of steps leading to the main door and inside, the church is wide and dramatic with mock archways in the roof in geometric patterns and two murals in the style of stained glass windows. Similar murals appear on the sides of the pulpit, which is bowl-shaped on a vivid yellow and brown rounded pedestal.

The centrepiece of the altar is not a crucifix but a modern pictorial representation of one, and behind it are the silver pipes of the organ.

The third church is notable not so much for its architectural style as for the two modern sculptures which stand outside. The basilica of Bonaria, in Viale Bonaria, is dedicated to the Virgin of Bonaria, the patron of sailors, which is appropriate because from the square in front there is a fine view over the gulf. Flights of grand steps on two sides match the imposing nineteenth-century façade, but there used to be a sanctuary on this spot in the fourteenth century which is another reason why the sailors' Saint is commemorated in its name. A legend says that a ship on its way from Spain to Italy was caught in a terrible storm and the sailors jettisoned everything they could find to save themselves. One particularly heavy chest refused to sink, and when it was washed ashore it was found to contain a statue of the madonna. The surviving sailors began building a sanctuary on the spot in her honour.

Today's basilica continues the sea-faring motif, for outside are a pair of modern statues in copper, each standing on a copper pedestal much larger than itself and designed in the form of waves. One figure is the madonna and the other a sailing ship, both the work of Francesco d'Aspro, a Sard. To commemorate Pope Paul VI's visit here in 1970 there is a statue of him in the porch. The interior of the church does not match up to the statues nor to its romantic legend, but it makes a good finale to Cagliari, because the sea and sea-faring people will be a recurring theme when you leave the capital and explore the rest of Sardinia.

4 Province of Cagliari

No generalisation will do to describe the Province of Cagliari, for it is not a cohesive slab of country but a collection of self-contained areas, each dealing with a separate facet of Sardinia's economy. On the map it is the southern wedge of the island, bulging out round its lower end with the enormous Gulf of Cagliari separating its western and eastern coastlines. But the oil-men and miners in their industrial setting have little in common with the pastoral farmers and their homes of mud and straw. The primitive fishing boats, just bundles of reeds tied together, punt through shallow lagoons while nearby is reclaimed swamp land with its irrigation channels and 1930s housing estates. The sleepy hill villages, built for safety slightly inland, look down with startled surprise at the twentieth-century tourist hotels on the shores below.

In a morning's drive history will move through 3,000 years and even the language will change. The obvious place to start from is the capital, for a good deal of the province can be explored using this as a base, particularly the region north of the city with its golden cornfields and lush vineyards. The road network begun by the Romans has been expanded to give today's motorist a good choice of alternative routes. It is a choice you will probably appreciate much later on, when you find yourself racketing along a gravel track which is the only means of reaching your destination.

The SS 131 is the main south-north highway of Sardinia and from Cagliari it runs across the Campidano plain with the first few miles containing the worst possible kind of industrial development. But most of the villages on this route are luckily off the dual-carriageway, so a mini-donkey pulling a maxi-cart waits patiently for a break in the cars to head off down a country lane where the traffic consists of a flock of sheep. Only at Monastir does the fertile agriculture become apparent. The surrounding meadows are full of red and yellow spring flowers and each field is protected by cypress trees or wind-breaks made of rushes. The palm trees look slightly out of place in this simple farming village named after the nearby ruined Camaldolesi monastery.

A few miles up the road at Nuraminis, most of the male population is already seated beneath the trees outside the municipal offices by 9.30 a.m. The sixteenth-century church is not in this main square but about 200 yards away and reached by a broad flight of steps. Its interior is two-style, part Catalan with an elegant star-vaulted roof above the apse and an ornate ceiling, and part simpler gothic. The roof and the bell-tower, with its working clock with faded numbers, are the oldest sections.

This is one of the typical villages of the Campidano, in which the Carthaginian style of house is still being built. It is made of sun-baked bricks of mud and straw and is easy to identify, if only because the finished product, the colour of cow dung and the same texture, looks a little more irregular than modern homes. From here more and more vineyards appear and the sun seems to shine more warmly and brightly on the grapes as you reach Sanluri, a town whose early history belies its current sleepy atmosphere, for it was the scene of a bitter conflict between the Aragonese and the Sards.

The castle in the centre of town was built by the Malaspina family and in 1345 Mariano IV, father of Eleonora, Sardinia's heroine, signed a peace treaty here with the King of Aragon, but sadly it was not to last long; the domination of the region passed from one side to the other. Eleonora's widower, Brancaleone, and his nephew, made an abortive attempt to capture the castle in 1408 and were caught by the Aragonese.

Later that century Don Martino, son of the King of Aragon, left his kingdom of Sicily, planning to subjugate and conquer for all time the province of Arborea. He won a decisive victory over the Genoese and their Sard allies at Alghero and then marched to Sanluri where, in 1499, he took on Aimerico, Visconte di Narbonna, Giudice of Arborea, who was married to the younger sister of the deceased Eleonora. The battle ended with 5000 Sards dead and a further 1000 inhabitants of Sanluri killed immediately afterwards. Flushed with victory, Don Martino intended to go on to conquer both Oristano and Iglesias but, as Tyndale puts it, 'enthralled by the charms of a Sanluri beauty, Don Martino sacrificed his health in every species of debauchery and died a victim to his follies.'

Today the fortress is the private home of Count Villasanta and is one of the more habitable castles despite its stern square battlements. It is surrounded by cypresses and geranium flowerbeds and from the ivy-covered courtyard where birds sing, steps lead up to a museum commemorating Italy's nineteenth-century revolutionaries; there is a second small military museum at ground floor level. The remainder of the castle rooms are surprisingly cosy, with red tiled floors, wooden ceilings and doors and furniture in handsome carved wood.

From Sanluri you can cut across to join the road that ten miles north brings you to Barumini. Nearby is one of the most important as well as more spectacular nuraghic sites in Sardinia, that of Su Nuraxi. It was largely unknown and unvisited until torrential rain in the winter of 1949 washed away the slopes of the hill and revealed not only the fortress but a spread-out village at its base. The major excavations were completed in 1954, but some of the village and its burial ground still lie beneath the grassy flower-strewn meadows.

Its history is necessarily partly conjecture, but the central truncated tower, now topped by grass, is said to date from the fifteenth century B.C., though its defensive loopholes and extra fortifications were added much later. Archaeologists say Su Nuraxi was attacked during the eighth century B.C., by whom it is not known, which resulted in another defensive layer being added. By now it had four towers at the corners, each with loop-holes for archers, in addition to the central tower whose courtyard had a well in case of siege, plus an outer wall.

All of this did not, however, save it from the Carthaginians, who in the second half of the sixth century B.C. captured it after a long siege and dismantled at least the top of the fortress as well as possibly burying the remainder when they left. A partisan account of events at that time has the inhabitants of the village forced into slavery by the Carthaginians and the few who managed to escape coming down from the mountains from time to time to try, unsuccessfully it would seem, to set fire to it. The Romans used dogs to discover the by-now camouflaged buildings and the pottery and coins they left behind seem to indicate habitation there, though by this time the villagers had disappeared.

In the absence of a guide, a torch is a useful addition to a tour of the fortress, whose interior is sinister and claustrophobic. There are tiny cells inside the main tower, which it is suggested were used as V.I.P. bedrooms, but in the light of their size this sounds improbable; on the other hand, one cell does have a floor insulated with cork for warmth. The feeling as you stand inside the courtyard is that the vast stone blocks will at any moment topple down upon you, and it is good to climb the rough steps to the top of the tower and a panoramic view. This is also the place to get an idea of the layout of the village.

The original nuraghic houses are circular, built with large blocks of stone and with niches in their thick walls for bedrooms. The Carthaginians extended these with tiny crammed hovels made of small stones held together by a clay cement. The primitive way of life is shown by the utilitarian household objects such as a rounded stone for pounding corn and a crude oven. The largest dwelling, variously called the Council Hall or the House of the Chief, is a good deal more opulent and the fishbone design above the entrance is a symbol of the nuraghic people and is continued in today's Sardinian handicraft designs.

Lizards and butterflies far outnumber humans visiting the ruins and it is a mile or two back into Barumini to change centuries and visit the sixteenth-century gothic church with its wooden ceiling and beautiful simplicity. The colours of the fourteenth-century triptych behind the altar are so well preserved it looks as though it was painted yesterday. A group of German tourists are also strolling about the church and break into a harmonious chant. They turn out to be priests in 'civvies', hence their spontaneous reaction.

One of the most delightful aspects of the setting is that opposite the church stands a renaissance country house, the two separated by a yew tree-lined path. The exterior of the empty building is delightfully crumbling with stone ornamentation on doors and windows. There are two big palm trees, a few fruit trees and the remains of a vegetable garden. The flowers grow wherever they please to their own pattern and at mid-day the smell of honeysuckle entices one to sit down and rest.

The scenery around Barumini is fairly hilly, but there is widespread cultivation with people tackling gargantuan fields with hoes. Just north of here, where the three provinces of Oristano, Nuoro and Cagliari meet, is the table-top basalt plateau called the Giara di Gesturi with a protected and little seen herd of wild horses. One reason why they are little seen is that the two-footed visitor has to climb 1000 feet or more to the plateau from the valley to stand even a chance of catching a glimpse of them; the visitor is further recommended to be on the top at dawn!

To return to Cagliari take a gentle meander down the N 128 cutting across to it a few miles south of Barumini from Villanova-Franca to Mandas, an agricultural centre and railway junction, then south through olive groves to Suelli, which in the Middle Ages became the seat of the Bishop of Barbagia when his own territories were too hostile to receive him. Its fourteenth-century romanesque church of San Giorgio has a sixteenth-century altar-piece by Pietro and Michele Cavaro and, like nearby Senorbi, Suelli is on the Trexenta Plain, so called because of the 30 villages that once comprised it. Senorbi also has an interesting parish church, with eighteenth-century wooden sculptures by Lonis, and it is the last hamlet of any interest before rejoining the main road at Monastir.

The south-eastern corner of the province has an encircl-
ing road and an empty central area occupied by rivers
and mountains rising to over 3000 feet. It would be too
strenuous to drive and enjoy it in one day, but it can
easily be tackled in two bites, either returning to Cagliari
or overnighting on the coast. One worthwhile trip just
half an hour's drive from the capital, is through the vineyards to Sinnai to see some of the loggia houses that are
a combination of Carthaginian and Roman architecture.
This does not necessarily mean that they are very old;
merely that the traditional way of building remains.

My guide lives in a modern house, the antithesis of
what we are about to see, but his hospitality is
traditional: a glass of home-made Malvasia that tastes
like a cross between mead and sherry. He is proud of his
modern paintings and furniture, but prouder still of an
old basket given him by his grandmother, showing the
designs, interwoven with scarlet wool, for which Sinnai is
famous.

It is a very different style of architecture on the next
call of the afternoon to a farmer and his wife who live in
a 'Roman' house built 30 years ago. All the rooms open
on to a loggia with marble columns, pretty ceiling and
tiled floor at one end of which is a 200 year old wooden
bridal chest, with birds and sun carvings, another craft,
like the basketwork, which is practised here today. This
house is full of Sard artefacts collected over the centuries,
but it is difficult to spot the difference between the gen-
uinely ancient, such as a collection of wooden spoons
with carved handles that came from great-grandmother,
and that which is modern and in everyday use such as a
wooden serving bowl with inset condiment spaces and a
carved lamb's head handle. The terracotta water jars and
the portable fire in a round brass bowl could be any age.

This home displays the wealth of its owners by having
an upper storey whose splendid non-livable reception
rooms are overflowing with damask-covered furniture.
Clearly the farmer and his wife never come up here
except to show visitors their treasures. The highlight of
the collection is in a tin box kept in the dining room
downstairs, and before the sideboard is even opened the

lace curtains are drawn, the shutters shut and the front door locked. The elaborate precautions are negated by the fact that the contents of the box cannot be successfully photographed in the now-darkened room so it is casually emptied on to a coffee table carried out into the back-yard.

The contents are an amazing private jewel collection. Most of it is gold and pearls such as filigree pendant ear-rings, a child's toy made of coral with three golden bells hanging from it, bracelets and necklaces, the whole a glistering display of workmanship that is far in advance of the modern imitations to be found in the shops. Once the jewels are safely packed away comes the hospitality in a sort of garage in which the farmer, like most of the people in this area, makes his own sweet red wine. In addition to the barrels he has a suspended bamboo tray on which to keep his cheeses and meat hooks with muslin cloths awaiting a side of this or that.

Back in the courtyard alongside the loggia there is an animated discussion about which flowers to pick to give the visitor and once the courtesies have been concluded it is on to an almost identical house, also fairly new, which is a replica of an old loggia house, now deserted, at the bottom of a broad bean and garlic patch. This host makes a light dry red wine and the gift is a bag of lem-ons, freshly picked from the trees that stand on either side of the front porch. The visiting could go on indefinitely and only the deepening dusk brings it to a gracious conclusion without having to offend the hospit-able Sinnai people by suggesting that one's wine capacity, especially when each glass is a different kind, must be limited if the drive back to Cagliari is to be safely made.

To take up the south-eastern circuit means retracing the trip from Sinnai until you can connect with the N 387 going north to Dolianova whose twelfth-century church of San Pantaleo has a fifth-century baptistry hewn from the rock. There is an almost Moorish look about the bell-tower while the rest of the church, rebuilt in the second half of the thirteenth century, is romanesque. The neigh-bouring village of Serdiana has the church of Santa Maria di Sibiola, now abandoned in a field surrounded by prickly pear hedges, which was founded in the twelfth century by the Benedictines of Saint-Victor at Marseilles, one of several this order built in Sardinia.

Continuing north from here for ten miles the road then branches at St Andrea Frius, the right-hand fork rising sharply through wooded scenery to S. Nicolo Gerrei and on to Villasalto which has the only antimony mine in Italy. This, though, is not the major interest. The curiosity of the village is its closed-in insular appearance, with all its dirt streets except one leading to a farmyard or a dead end.

These people are too poor to paint their grey granite houses, save for a touch of blue or pink or yellow round the windows. Finally one person is found who can read, understand the map and give directions to the only exit east. It is a rough gravel road which drops straight down, almost as though you have fallen out of Villasalto! No wonder two graphic signs warn 'Strada Dissestata' and 'Curva Pericoloso'. You do need a cool head, but it is worth it because at the bottom of the nerve-racking descent – only three miles though it seems like 30 – is a secret valley surrounded by high hills which effectively enclose it.

The gravel road continues alongside the tranquil River Flumendosa with occasionally a brief, flat, narrow strip of market gardening, mainly vines. This secret paradise lasts until San Vito, when the tarmac road starts and the valley broadens out with bamboo hedges protecting citrus orchards in an area of reclaimed land. Muravera, while not actually at the river mouth, has all the hall-marks of a seaside place, with boats parked in forefronts or passing by on car roof-racks. The road north from here would bring you out of Cagliari Province, passing the thirteenth-century ruined Castle of Quirra and the romanesque thirteenth-century church of San Nicolo before crossing the limestone massif called Salto di Quirra.

But to continue the south-eastern circuit, turn sharply south from Muravera on the only road which leaves a little row of hills between itself and the sea and a line of much bigger hills inland, looking hazy, mysterious and almost purple in the late afternoon sun. This road could take you cross-country to Cagliari, but there is a side road at a hamlet called S. Priamo which takes you through the reclaimed agricultural land with its identical neat farmhouses. Eucalyptus and baby pines join bamboo to protect the orchards and there is the serrated edge inland of the Setti Fratelli mountains, rising to more than 3000 feet, and visible almost as far as Villasimius.

Four miles along a narrow peninsula is Capo Carbonara overlooking the tiny island of Cavoli with its lighthouse. Its modern name is derived from the quantity of wild cabbages said to grow there, but in olden times it was called Ficaria. From Villasimius the 25-mile run west to Cagliari is the playground of the capital with increasing tourist development all the way. Capo Boi is typical, with its grand hotel. There is a private beach with bamboo shades, deckchairs and changing rooms, a large heated swimming pool, tennis courts and lots of ground. Most of the early summer customers are Germans who have brought their cars with them by sea.

This coast road is a picturesque one and on a Sunday morning the Cagliarese are driving out in their hundreds, carrying boats, deckchairs, parasols, tables and so on, but apparently no food, for a mere three hours later they are jamming the roads to get home for lunch. From Capo Boi the first little resort is Solanus with a pretty beach, an hotel and a stumpy sentinel tower on a headland, which is a feature of almost every cove along the way.

At Geremeas the uniform development begins and it gets more crowded the nearer you are to the capital. Sadly, it seems the dustmen will not make the trek down to the actual seaside villas, which means the owners climb up to deposit their rubbish in areas called Divieto Discardia. These are, unfortunately, lay-bys on the roadside and create a distinctly disagreeable impression on the passing motorist.

Cala Regina is a tiny, stony cove and from here prickly pears, tamarisk and eucalyptus make their appearance until, at Capitana, the scenery opens out into a lush plain of corn and mini-orchards. This is almost in the suburbs of Cagliari and it remains only to pass through Quartu Sant'Elena which bravely tries to retain its

individuality. It makes sweets and has the Festival of the Almonds to exhibit them, and also filigree buttons for the national costumes. It also has, hidden somewhere in its dreary streets, the thirteenth-century romanesque church of San Pietro built in the cemetery of another. The centre of the city is a few minutes' drive and you would now be wise to pack your bags and leave the capital, for the remainder of the province, the bulging west, will require overnight stops en route.

Driving south-west on the main coast road, the first place of interest is Villa d'Orri whose mansion of the same name has a history that has been interwoven with Sardinia since its owners, the Villehermosas, arrived here in the sixth century. It was for a long time the home of the Kings of Savoy, having been courteously vacated for royalty by the family, and although it is not officially open to the public I receive an invitation to drop in on the same night as Sant'Efisio is expected and find that a large uninvited crowd is also there, at least in the grounds and courtyards. Gaining entry to the house is quite another matter. It seems a sensible idea to follow these smartly-clad Sard visitors who park their cars at the end of the driveway and walk confidently pass the walls and through archways into a beautiful inner courtyard.

Once there, however, they disperse to wander through the magnificent gardens or sit chatting on the courtyard benches. No one has the slightest intention of actually going in and there is no door or bell or visible means of entry. I am finally directed round the corner, through the kitchen yard and into the servants' quarters where a female major-domo, after a hurried search for a bunch of keys, sets off with me via kitchens and storerooms, briefly back into the courtyard, through a loggia, each door being locked behind us and finally up a flight of stone steps to the open front door.

The Marquese Julia Villehermosa is expecting an indeterminate number of dinner guests including a medley of family relations already there, and explains that this is the one night of the year when the house is closed off so that the general public who have come to see the Saint are restricted to the courtyard and family chapel. Nevertheless, she has time to give me a private tour of the Villa. It is now a scheduled monument and is largely nineteenth-century though there are foundation sections dating from the twelfth. Its interior is not beautiful, except for fine ceiling paintings some of which were restored by the Marquese's late father-in-law after Second World War damage when part of the roof caved in.

Carlo Felice, King of Sardinia, who spent about five years on the island, left behind a few little mementoes of his stay at Villa d'Orri, including fans and miniatures and an enormous four-poster bed which, says the Marquese feelingly, is quite the most uncomfortable bed she has ever slept on. The Queen's bedroom is at the other end of the house and a portrait of Maria-Christina there could explain why! She had, it seems, many qualities, but beauty was certainly not one of them.

Today's Villehermosas are an extraordinary mixture of ancient and modern, aristocratic aunts and cousins speaking nothing but Sard while their offspring, informally clad, practise their English. More than this, there has been an infusion of American blood after centuries of first cousins marrying each other, for the Marquese is from Missouri and met her husband in Paris when she was an airline hostess. Not a word of Italian, much less Sard, did she speak when she arrived in Sardinia 13 years ago to meet for the first time her husband's twin brother, his other two brothers and the rest of the family. They lived for a year at Villa d'Orri before moving to a modern villa a few miles away.

Now the Marquese and her trilingual 12-year-old son live in Cagliari, for a tragic reason. Four years ago her husband was kidnapped and murdered by bandits and she feels that life in the city is safer for the boy. Apart from his linguistic abilities, Billy looks like the all-American boy and so do some of his cousins, that is the children of the Marquese's brother, who for the last two years has been managing the estate. Her late husband ran a construction company with capital realised by the sale of some of the family land to the oil refineries. Before that the acreage stretched north of Cagliari to Decimomannu, south to beyond Sarroch and inland to the mountains. When the land is finally reparcelled, by tradition, to the children of the four brothers, it will be a small bite each compared with the original 50,000 or 60,000 acres.

In its early days Villa d'Orri was used only as a winter residence because of the threat of malaria. Now it is occupied the year round but has those qualities so often found in stately homes; fearfully hot in summer and terribly cold in winter. Spring is not exactly comfortable, either, and the Marquese is muffled in warm clothing as we go out on to the terrace, where the smell of jasmine wafts across and from the courtyard below there is the excited chatter of the crowd. Her guests are awaiting her, and I must await Sant'Efisio whose journey to this point has already been described.

Beyond Villa d'Orri are the disfiguring oil refineries and uniform new homes for workers at Sarroch, making one rush past, instead of searching for the nearby nuraghe Domu'e d'Orcu. The mountains rise mistily to more than 2500 feet inland and around Pula are vineyards and orchards and tomato-filled greenhouses interspersed with the fine new villas of the oil executives. In the little town the bunting is out to greet the Saint, expected later that day, and the narrow lane to his church lined with eucalyptus trees is a busy one as holidaymakers and pilgrims walk, drive or ride the mile or two to Nora.

The church, dating from 1089 with a rebuilt façade, is delightfully simple, its narrow nave lined with thick pillars and rounded arches. The few pews are crowded and in the porch sit the old men. For this once-a-year occasion the stallholders outside are selling 'Welcome to Sardinia' records, leather bags, belts and wallets, a variety of cork items such as bottle and glass holders, trays and book covers, and a variety of things to eat such as nuts, sausages and roasting piglets. It is a marvellous mixture of religion and commercialism, with a clear indication that the arrivals will enjoy both.

Sant'Efisio makes an annual pilgrimage here, because he was martyred by the Romans on the nearby small peninsula of Sa Punta de Coloro, where they built Nora known as the mother city of Sardina. Fortunately the eleventh-century Sards hid the Saint's relics from the invading Saracens, and Nora itself remained neglected and undisturbed until 25 years ago. The official facts have it that excavations have so far uncovered six acres of the city, to reveal temples, houses, paved streets, mosaics and an excellent drainage system.

A delightful – if partisan – tale tells of how the first play to be performed in the newly discovered amphitheatre escaped disaster through the Saint's intervention. The play and theatre were both prepared in something of a rush, neither were judged to be really ready come the première when, in addition, it was pouring with rain. Sant'Efisio stopped the rain, arranged for the moon to come out, made certain the actors knew their parts and finally ensured the working of the untried stage lighting. Since which success, Nora could hardly fail to become one of the Sards' favourite historical places.

The site is certainly a splendid one, on the top of a narrow peninsula, thus fulfilling the requirements of the Phoenicians who first established themselves here and who preferred either islands or a defensible promontory like Nora. The Carthaginians were the next occupiers, but the city really came into its own with the Romans who built a road to link it with Karalis (Cagliari) and Sulcis. The city never recovered from the invasions of the Vandals and the attacks of the Saracens, but this has one great advantage for today's visitors: the only addition since Roman times is the Spanish tower of Coltellazzo, built by Philip II in the sixteenth century and now used as a lighthouse as it commands the view of the Bays of Cagliari and Teulada.

Nora does not have the benign green prospect of some of Sardinia's archaeological sites, but there are occasional little flowers struggling to survive on the rocky foreshore and the smell of pines early in the morning. A diligent paddle fails to reveal the bits of the city that are said to be still submerged beneath the waves.

Within a mile or so of Pula you will find yourself back in the twentieth century, because the next section of the coastline is highly developed tourism set among the pine forests, with luxurious villas standing back on the slopes of the macchia-covered hills. Santa Margherita marks the start, with a de-luxe holiday village as well as a number of hotels, and the holiday scene continues with varying degrees of concentration the ten or so miles to Bithia, whose Punic-Roman ruins, mentioned by Ptolemy and dating from the fourth century B.C., were exposed by a storm in 1933, though some of the town remains buried on the beach. The Pisan Torre di Chia, built in the seventeenth century, stands guard.

This is the beginning of the Costa del Sud, a picturesque detour off the main road where very smart villas are thinly scattered. It is not, however, always easy to reach the sea, either because the villa owner has blocked off access, or because the road is suddenly several hundred feet up or back from the shore, and separated from it by bushy low scrub which in May is almost autumnal in colours of russetts and browns. The scenery gradually becomes less rugged and has run down to a flat plain by the time Porto di Teulada is reached, a rather grandiose name for a few fishing cottages and a handful of boats in a sheltered cove.

Teulada itself lies about four miles inland, back on the main road and in an area famed for its oranges and lemons. There are vineyards and almond orchards in the surrounding countryside as well as the first appearance of bamboo, and the hill town with its narrow steep streets and Moorish-Spanish look wears a somnolent pre-summer air. Like many towns in Sardinia, it was founded by the inhabitants of a coastal place, in this case Tegula, from whence its people fled to escape Saracen and Barbary raids.

Eight miles away on the same road is Domus de Maria, where the Semitic God of Marriage, Bes, was worshipped and, it is alleged, helped girls to find husbands. Retracing the drive to Teulada and continuing north there is little to be seen except the pastoral life: a donkey loaded with enormous double panniers of grass, farmers carrying two-pronged hoes, and the occasional flock of sheep or goats. The flat plain also contains an army base and military camp which in no way hinders passing motorists.

Before turning left to Sant'Antioco there is Tratalias whose church of Santa Maria was consecrated in 1213 when it was a cathedral and the little village was the See of the diocese. It has since been variously altered by the addition of Tuscan, Gothic and Lombard styles. Nearby is the Lake of Monte Pranu formed by a barrage on the River Palmas. All along this shoreline are the shallow stagnos, or lagoons, used either for fishing or saline works, and the largest and final one before leaving the mainland is Stagno di San Caterina.

The island of Sant'Antioco, 11 miles long and four miles wide, is reached via a causeway originally built by the Carthaginians and reinforced by the Romans who added a bridge and really put the place on the map. They called it Plumbea after the lead mines in the district and founded the town of Sulcis, now largely submerged, but whose name was extended to cover the south-west corner of Sardinia where it is still in use. Sant'Antioco flourished under both the Phoenicians and the Romans but, like other places on the island, it suffered badly under the Vandals and Saracens who between them seem to have annihilated the population and obliterated the villages.

Today's inhabitants are descended from Genoese refugees from Tunisia and it is they who have given Sant'Antioco and its neighbouring island of San Pietro a distinctive flavour as well as a dialect all its own. Twentieth-century man, like the Romans, saw the importance of the minerals and just before the Second World War built a harbour to handle the output. The port is busy and industrial, in contrast to the sleepy modern town whose main street, offering just two simple restaurants, is lined with oleanders trimmed into a pleasing continuous high 'hedge'.

Up the hill is the old historic area with the church of Sant'Antioco, built in 1102 by the Benedictines of Saint-Victor at Marseilles, whose catacombs are the resting place of the Saint after whom the town is named. The most severe torture failed to kill him, so the story goes, and his frustrated executioners finally threw him into the sea to drown. That failed too, and Antioco floated ashore at Sulcis where he converted the people and became their bishop. A cheerful pig-tailed girl leads me by the hand to the entrance of the church whose interior is simple with rounded arches of mellow brown stone.

Its cavernous height is a contrast to the catacombs where the guide, wearing tennis shoes, has a Botticelli face and is all of nine years of age, just the right height to avoid hitting his head on the low doorways that link the tombs. Children seem to be a feature of the historical sights on Sant'Antioco, for round the corner and further up Fortino Hill from the church, there is an even smaller boy who is the son of the museum custodian and used by his father to illustrate in graphic macabre detail the child sacrifices that took place long before Antioco arrived. The old man tells with relish the story of Moloch who sacrificed the first-born of patrician families to Tanit and Baal, pointing to the terracotta urns and stone sarcophagi to indicate where the ashes went.

Across the road in the necropolis the tale becomes even more dramatic. This ruin is about the size of an English field, with a football pitch at the bottom in use on a Saturday afternoon. There is some kind of drainage furrow running down the sloping middle and here the specialities are skeletons, left in the positions in which they were found, but with wooden covers to protect them. Many have urns beside them and the guide explains that these jars were broken just below the neck in order that the ashes could be poured in. The language barrier prevents a detailed discussion with him on why there are both bones and ashes.

A treasure of which he is particularly proud is hidden beneath a layer of branches and consists of two of the finest urns, still half buried. The place where the childrens' throats were slit is pointed out, and so is the enclosure atop the hill where the bodies were cremated. The tour ends by crawling through the tombs, or possibly dungeons, that have been built beneath the necropolis.

After this gloomy investigation into the island's past, it is pleasant to drive into the countryside via the gravel road, north to the only other place of any size, the port of Calasetta, six miles from the town of Sant'Antioco. Prickly pear hedges protect the vineyards that produce a good dessert wine, so it is no surprise to learn that Calasetta's annual jamboree is the Feast of the Grapes after the September harvest.

The village, you could hardly call it more, has a charming and unusual sparkling white church that looks like a mosque, and all its straight streets make a geometrical square pattern. The main ones are wide enough for two cars to pass carefully, avoiding the water run-off in the centre, and all run down the hill to the port, round the corner of which is a little bay with a cluster of new villas. The harbour comes alive half a dozen times a day with the departure of the car ferry to the neighbouring island of San Pietro, and taking the last boat just before 6 p.m., it is warm enough on a mid-May evening to pass the 30-minute crossing on deck.

San Pietro's port is much bigger than Calasetta, although the island is smaller than Sant'Antioco, a mere six miles long and five wide. Its harbour of Carloforte has two boat services, one to the mainland where the crossing to Portovesme takes 40 minutes and runs ten times a day from dawn until late evening, and the other from the neighbouring isle, where the ferry ponderously reverses to tie up at the end of the pier, disgorging only three cars and a dozen people. The Saint after whom this island is named is supposed to have been shipwrecked here on his way to Cagliari and to have taught the inhabitants how to catch fish with harpoons and nets, most practical for a Saint.

The Romans called the island Accipitrum after the number of hawks they found, but their influence here was much less than on neighbouring Sant'Antioco and in fact San Pietro, after its colonisation by Carthage and Rome, remained deserted for hundreds of years until the mid-eighteenth century, when by a strange quirk it was repeopled from Tunisia. Why the King of Sardinia, Carlo Emanuele III, should have heeded the pleas of a remote Genoese colony on the island of Tabarca off the Tunisian coast is not clear. But the colony's request to take over San Pietro, on the grounds that life in Tabarca was be-

coming increasingly non-viable as tiresome Barbary neighbours carried off their womenfolk and children, was
granted in 1738.

They had hardly taken up occupation, however, when
the Barbary pirates landed and removed most of the new
inhabitants as slaves back to Tunisia. Generous King
Carlo ransomed his prospective colonists and formally
established them at Carloforte in 1750, hence the name
of the town and the grand statue of the king in the main
piazza. Unfortunately the immigrants' problems were not
over, and it was not long before they were defending their
island, unsuccessfully, against a French fleet under
Admiral Truguet in early 1793. The valiant new Sards
burned their town to prevent it falling into the hands of
the enemy.

When that particular enemy was disposed of, the Tunisian pirates returned and carried on with their slave-trad-
ing, and for nearly 20 years the poor islanders were subject to continual raids with their toll of property and people. When peace finally came, the colony, still less than
70 years of age, turned its attention to the fishing lessons
taught by its Saint. Tunny fishing, it is true, had come
to the notice of the Aragon government during their
domination of Sardinia in the sixteenth century, but San
Pietro took to it with enthusiasm – with the help of Ligu-
rian fishermen – if only because there was little else to
live on and the shoals of tunny passed their door in May
and June.

The 'mattanza', from the Spanish *matar* to slay, is a
concentrated bloody slaughter in which nets are laid and
the tunny lured to the central *camera della morte* (death
cell). The head fisherman, called rais after the Arab word
for chief, decides by looking through a glass-bottomed
boat when sufficient fish have been collected and gives the
signal. The nets are pulled in and the men in the waiting
tight circle of fishing boats spear each giant fish manually
and drag the catch into the boats. It is transferred to the
tonnara, the fishing station, to be scaled, gutted and sent
to market all in one annual fast-moving sea harvest.

This is by no means the only fishing activity on San
Pietro. The smart green and white boats with short masts

and striped bowsprits bring back the lobsters, sardines and prawns which make up the menus in the waterfront restaurants, with the addition of their own special fish soup flavoured with basil, nuts and garlic. Vegetable couscous, an inheritance from Tabarca, is the regular Sunday lunch of the visitors who come over from the mainland (paying little more than the price of a coffee for their fare) to join the islanders on their traditional promenade.

The merry crowd strolls along the harbour-side, with its oleanders, palm trees and marble statue to Carlo Emanuele III showing the king rescuing a man, woman and child, then turns into the Corso Repubblica and the pedestrians-only Piazza del Repubblica. The houses in pastel shades look freshly colour-washed and the balconies have special wooden frames on which to hang the laundry. Chirping birds in cages which hang outside front doors add to the charm. Those who fail to get a table in the handful of restaurants here can walk a couple of hundred yards from the jetty to the hotel, where the previous evening I had been met by a literally open-arm-ed manager who showed an extraordinary anxiety that the car should not be parked in one of the several empty parking bays outside his door.

It all seemed rather curious, but at dinner the mystery was solved: the parking places had been reserved for a splendid country wedding party, 50-strong, including grandmothers and children, who all sat down to supper. After a couple of speeches the happy pair, who were, endearingly, neither pretty, handsome nor young, made a circuit of the dining room to offer everyone, including hotel guests, a piece of the five-tier wedding cake and a traditional good luck gift of a handful of almonds wrapp-ed in a paper flower.

Carloforte lies on the east coast of San Pietro and to tour the island from here there are three simple routes: south, north and west. Heading south takes you past the Observatory, (one of six set up in 1899 on the 39th para-llel by the International Geodetic Survey) and past the San Vittorio tower and the saltpans, alongside which is a narrow canal containing more than 100 little boats. This is the most populous end, which does not mean it is overcrowded, but new villas are going up, there is a camping area in tamarisk trees and at La Caletta there is a beach area with an hotel.

To reach La Punta at the northern tip of the island, all of three miles as the crow flies from Caloforte, the road hugs the seashore fairly closely and the only landmark is a wooded hill called the Moor's Watch Tower which, because it is 600 feet high, was used as a look-out for possible Barbary invasions in the old days. The western route, grandly called Strade Importante, is an exceedingly rough narrow gravel track winding through macchia scrub with tiny pockets of cultivation where the vines are protected by low stone walls.

Along the way are strange volcanic-type rocks with eroded holes in them and at the end of the trip is a lighthouse, a military post and the sea far below. The coast is full of inlets, grottoes and cliffs which can be reached only by boat. It is anything but hospitable, in contrast to the inhabitants, and the longer one spends there the more possible is it to believe in Saint Peter's shipwreck as well as to wonder how the early raiders succeeded in getting ashore at all.

Portovesme, the mainland ferry terminus from San Pietro, merges into Portoscuso, whose quay loads metal ores. Both places have heavy concentrated industry, and there seems to be a total absence of any signposts, which leads to an unscheduled detour south to Carbonia. This mining town was established by Mussolini, with its broad streets laid out at right angles, each workers's house with its own garden, and an imposing Piazza Roma with theatre, town hall and other public buildings. The only ancient touch, a Phoenician and Carthaginian fort atop nearby Sirai Hill, is likely to be overlooked by tourists since the fine new road was built to speed them north through sharp mining hills to the red scarred open castings outside Iglesias.

The earliest accounts of this town date from the mid-thirteenth century, and it was fought over first by the Pisans and the Gherardesca family who owned the whole area, and later by the Kings of Aragon. The Pisans had

surrounded Iglesias with walls and towers against an
expected invasion by their arch-enemies and it came in
1323 when the Infante Don Alfonso, son of the Aragonese
King, landed at Sulcis with a fleet of 500 vessels and a
large military force. In addition he had local reinforce-
ments led by the Giudice of Arborea waiting in the Gulf
of Palmas.

But any thoughts he may have entertained of an easy
victory were soon dispelled. The town garrison of 200
cavalry and 1000 infantry held out for six months and
when, in desperation, they sent their women, children and
old people outside the walls to become prisoners and,
hopefully, to be fed, Don Alfonso sent them back inside
again. His attacks never succeeded, he lost 12,000 men
and he had to wait for the weary defenders of Iglesias to
surrender. A century later the inhabitants swung to the
other side, became vehement loyalists to the Aragon
crown and even put up their own 'ransom' to bail out
their bankrupt king who was planning to raise money by
handing over the feudal rights of the town to another
overlord.

Iglesias used to be aptly called Argentaria, from the
silver the Pisans mined in the neighbourhood. It remains
the most important mining area in Italy, including that
country's only supply of gold, plus iron, zinc and lead.
Its current name dates from the Middle Ages and the
many churches it had then, most of which are still standing. The cathedral, whose foundations were built in 1285,
reflects the town's turbulent history showing as it does
both Pisan and Aragonese influences. Its interior has high
gothic arches but its façade is mixed with romanesque
and the bell in the tower was cast by Andrea Pisano in
1337.

The ecclesiastical importance of the town went up and
down. The bishopric was transferred from Tratalias to
Iglesias in 1503, incorporated with the archbishopric of
Cagliari in 1691 and in 1763 again became a separate
See. The cathedral stands in the pedestrians-only Piazzet-
ta del Municipio and no traffic is allowed, either, in the
narrow streets leading away from the square or indeed
anywhere in the old town, which makes it a very pleasant

place to wander around. But it requires some determination to find the churches.

Among the gems are San Francesco, on Via Satta, which is gothic fifteenth century; Santa Chiara, in Piazza Manzoni, which is thirteenth-century romanesque; Nostra Signora di Valverde, in Via Valverde, which is late thirteenth century and has a similar façade to that of the cathedral; and the enchanting Nostra Signora di Buon Cammino which sits white and pretty atop a suburban hill giving a view of the surroundings. Almost the only modern part of Iglesias is the Piazza Quintino Sella, though even that has some old walls peeping out of a corner. Sella is said to have developed and improved the wines on the island, but his bust mounted on a lump of rock in the centre of the square seems to have been transposed into a mining theme, which is logical for a town whose annual festival in October includes an exhibition of silver and minerals.

From Iglesias it is worth taking a detour east to Domusnovas, one of the villages owned by Count Ugolino della Gherardesca, who is famous for his part in Dante's Inferno. In 1838 Balzac passed through while investigating a scheme he had devised for refining silver refuse, in which he was forestalled by a Marseilles mining company. The Gherardesca castle of Acquafredda is several miles distant, south of Siliqua. It was built in the thirteenth century; Ugolino's rebellious son Guelfo was kept a prisoner there and it was taken by the Pisans in 1258.

But the purpose in visiting Domusnovas is not this famous family, but – a mile to the north – the Grotto of San Giovanni, which is quite a surprise because it is a natural rock tunnel. Its early use was probably as a fortress and refuge, for there are man-made walls visible at both ends and the remains of a chapel. At the other side the tarmac ends abruptly, the track gets steeper and rougher, the mountains close in and at about 2000 feet and one hour later, a solitary man working at a remote tiny power station in a spot ominously called Perdu Carta insists that the road ahead is impassable. There is little doubt that he is right, so the adventurous detour ends where it began, back through the tunnel to

Domusnovas, and from thence to Iglesias to rejoin the main highway north.

Beyond the double lakes of Monteponi and Punta Gennarta the road climbs to the pass of Genna Bogai, which seems much higher than its 1500 feet and drops down on the other side to the hamlet of San Angelo with, shortly afterwards, a totally unmarked track leading to the Roman Temple of Antas where the island god, Sardus Pater, is said to have been worshipped. There is room in this narrow valley for only the road and the River Antas, but after Fluminimaggiore the mountains stand back to give you a breather before tackling another pass which ends the switchback part of the journey.

The little town of Arbus is spreadeagled on the hillside to give you a view over the plain to Guspini, three miles further on, where it is pouring with rain so sightseeing is restricted to interiors. The fifteenth-century Aragonese-gothic church of San Nicola has a façade lightened by a rose window, while inside it is sombre and austere. Teenagers out of school are flocking into ice-cream parlours, of which there seem to be very many, and it requires several sets of directions to find the only trattoria. The standard of food here, including raw broad bean salad, is very high, and then one discovers that the Sard proprietor and his Spanish wife were, until a few months ago, managing one of London's fashionable restaurants. It is the only time I hear fluent English spoken in a small country town.

There are four possible routes from here: travelling 15 miles west on a narrow twisting road to Costa Verde via Montevecchio, centre of a mining region; continuing north direct to Oristano; south-east to Villacidro to visit the Spendula waterfall and drive through orange and lemon groves; or east to San Gavino Monreale, which has the largest lead foundry in Italy and, a few miles north on a side road, the ruined castle of Monreale. This castle was one of the fortresses of the Giudice of Arborea, controlling by its position all communications between Oristano and Cagliari, and Dona Teresa, the wife of Infante Don Alfonso, stayed here while her husband attacked Cagliari after his long-drawn out siege of Iglesias.

The castle is in fact nearer to Sardara, where the Romans built a spa they called Thermae Neapolitanae, now known as the Terme di Sardara. There are five hot springs of sodium bicarbonate water and the charming setting is amid pine and eucalyptus woods. Though the steam is rising the baths are not yet open for the season, but a private tour of the cavernous place is possible. From here to Oristano on the main ss 131 highway is just 30 miles.

5 Oristano

Oristano, the capital of a newly formed province, has somehow managed to find the only dry firm ground for miles around. Its watery situation includes the mouth of one of Sardinia's rivers, shallow stagnos or lagoons both north and south, and alongside it is the enormous gulf of the same name. This marshy swamp area had certain advantages in the early days, for precarious as it may sound, the little islands that were scattered among the lagoons were the only possible hiding places from the Vandals and Saracens. Indeed the town was founded in 1070 by refugees who fled here from the Roman town of Tharros a few miles away on the peninsula that shelters the bay. Of the original settlement of Othoca there is no trace.

Today's city is one of prosperous merchants with a decidedly middle-class flavour, but appearances can deceive and once a year Oristano breaks out in mediaeval jousting. The choice of this particular period in history for its annual jamboree is not accidental, for it is a reminder of their golden age, the age of the island's greatest heroine, Eleonora d' Arborea whose exploits some say rank with those of Joan of Arc, although she is hardly known outside Sardinia.

Eleonora, who lived in the fourteenth century, balked at nothing, whether it was leading her troops into battle, negotiating treaties to her own advantage, making alliances that would benefit her region or laying down a code of laws that was centuries ahead of its time. She was Giudice of Arborea, Oristano was her home, and its inhabitants take a quiet understated pride in their heroine. Her predecessors, however, did not make an auspicious beginning to this golden age and indeed one luckless fellow who was a Giudice in the twelfth century nearly wrecked any chance of independence and freedom for his people.

His name was Barisone, and in 1165 having got wind of an invasion from two neighbouring Giudici, Logudoro and Cagliari, far from staying to fight he took himself off to Cabras to seek help from the Genoese. His Sard enemies, treaty-bound to the Pisans, in the meantime helped themselves liberally to booty and prisoners in his territory. Not only did the Genoese lend Barisone their moral support, but they passed on his request to their Emperor that he should be given the title of King of Sardinia.

Emperor Frederick, a man of changeable moods, promptly removed the Sardinian crown from his uncle's head and placed it on Barisone at Pavia, in Italy. This turned out to be a premature move, because when it came to the question of tribute to the Emperor, Barisone the Bankrupt could not pay and retained his title only by promising never to set foot in his kingdom until he had paid his debts. His efforts to raise the cash failed and he lost his title to the Pisans. However, unluckily for the Sards, he remained Giudice of Arborea and in 1168 received permission to return to Oristano. Not that he had any intention of doing anything for his people, he was merely trying to consolidate his diminished position. The visit was an abortive one, he returned to Genoa, went back to Sardinia in 1171 and three years later capitulated completely and handed over the territory to the Pisans, spending his remaining years quarrelling with the other Giudici.

At this point there is a gap in the affairs of Oristano until the emergence of Mariano IV. He had been brought up a royal prince at the Court of Aragon and when the Giudice of Arborea died in 1346 without children, Mariano was nominated his successor. For a time it looked as though he would be no better than Barisone. He was a mediaeval double-dealer, professing ardent loyalty to the distant Aragonese King while he actually defeated the Aragonese on his own ground in 1347. His request in 1352 to be given Alghero was turned down and his turn-coat policies led to almost continuous warfare for the next couple of decades.

Meanwhile Mariano was endeavouring to cement local alliances by marrying his daughter Eleonora to Brancaleone Doria, a nobleman from an important, wealthy and influential Sardinian family. That did not work out too well either, for his son-in-law promptly deserted to the Aragonese in an early battle. Luckily, his son Ugone IV was on hand to successfully beat off the enemy and it was Ugone who succeeded, following his father's death from the plague in 1376. But Mariano had done one thing: he had told his family of plans for a Code of Laws. These plans might have been executed by Ugone, but his murder in 1383 was the cue for an uprising, led by those who hoped to eradicate the entire family.

But they had reckoned without Eleonora, who gathered a few loyal troops, rode at their head and routed the rebels. While her infant son Frederick was officially nam-ed Giudice, Eleonora intended to be the controlling force. Her cowardly husband, Brancaleone, fled to the Court of Aragon, where he became virtually a prisoner and she took over the Arborea castles and had the population swear allegiance to the young boy. Furthermore, she sent to the King of Aragon asking for help to restore order in her territory – a crafty political move.

The King, however, already alarmed by Eleonora's antics, delayed sending the promised help and finally insisted on keeping young Frederick as hostage. Brancaleone was sent back to Arborea with instructions to get pro-Aragonese treaties signed, a quite impossible task. His wife refused all pleas to cooperate and went on fighting the Aragonese for two more years until she judg-ed her position sufficiently advantageous to negotiate a treaty on her own terms.

By the time the treaty was signed, in 1388, some of the benefits had been whittled away, but Eleonora still sec-ured her territories and her husband's release and he, spurred on by his courageous and intrepid wife, for once took her side and a couple of years later was in the forefront of more battles against the Aragonese. Eleonora then persuaded the Genoese to give assistance and, with their fleet, successfully subdued the whole of her province while Brancaleone captured Sassari, one of the treaty's original concessions which had been subsequently removed from the terms.

You would have imagined this continual state of warfare would have left room for little else, but Eleonora was also a politician and administrator, and it is for this latter ability that she is particularly remembered, for she left behind a system of government that would be copied by the rest of Sardinia and that was to last for centuries, the notable Carta di Logu, or Code of Laws, so called after Logudoro. What she took from her father's unwritten ideas is not known, but the Code was first published in 1395 and less than 30 years later was in use throughout most of the island, save for certain towns too vulnerable to the threat of invasion to have time for civil laws.

Eleonora's Carta is a remarkable document and can be seen, with a little difficulty, in the University library in Cagliari where I lined up with the students for opening time, got an entry ticket, filled out forms in triplicate and waded through a number of books about the lady before the treasure was brought out, in bound form, with fine script. I had expected an ornate scroll with gold lettering, this is tight-knit writing, very workmanlike and runs to 198 chapters. It is amazingly comprehensive, setting out legal proceedings, and criminal and civil law, but above all it is designed to solve the problems of the day, which is what makes it so fascinating.

The question of agriculture, for instance, was a vital one, so in order to prevent sheep stealing the Carta ruled that the possessor of any skin had to be able to prove its origin, no easy thing to accomplish. Fire was a great risk in those days, and here the laws were fairly severe, but with very precise applications. If you lit a fire anywhere in the countryside during the summer there was a mighty fine to pay. If that fire caused damage you lost an ear. If it was proved to be arson the fine was so stupendous that you were unlikely to be able to pay and so lost your right hand. Urban arson was punishable – appropriately enough – by death by burning. But it was, of course, exceedingly difficult to find the culprit, especially in rural areas, so a clause in the Carta provided for community punishment, in which all the men of the nearest village had to combine to pay the fine – a real mediaeval deterrent.

But most important of all, the Carta expressed a spirit of humanitarianism. The examples just quoted might sound harsh in today's terms, but the great majority of offences were payable by fine and at no time were the wives and children of the guilty party included or their possessions or property confiscated. The insistence on not penalising families and making one crime an excuse for a witch hunt was a remarkable achievement in those times. Says Tyndale: 'The framing of a body of laws so far in advance of those of other countries, where greater civilisation existed, must ever be the brightest ornament in the diadem of the Giudicessa.'

Sandinia's heroine died of plague in 1403 or 1404 and her second son had a regency for only three or four years before he, too, died and Eleonora's widower, Brancaleone, claimed the Giudice. She is, quite rightly, commemorated in Oristano, but rather as a member of the family and a friend. Naturally the piazza containing her statue is named after her, but it is not a very magnificent monument, nor is it all that old, being the work of the Florentine sculptor, Ulisse Cambi, in 1881. Our heroine is in marble, clutching a copy of the Carta du Logu and raising a declamatory arm. Lions sit at each corner and inset panels depict Eleonora's victories both in war and peace-time.

A few minutes' walk from here is her house, only it was not her house at all but was built in the sixteenth century, like the Doria House in Alghero which bears no relation to that family and was also put up centuries later. Finding the house in Via Parpaglia requires the assistance of a passer-by, who points out a gracious renaissance building so neglected that weeds are growing out of the first-floor shuttered windows. Perhaps a plaque would be in order, and certainly the attractive stone carved window facings could be restored before they fall apart.

Piazza Eleonora is linked by the pedestrians-only Corso Umberto I to Piazza Roma, the centre of Oristano, which with its trees and flowerbeds and through traffic, is dominated by the Torre San Cristoforo, sometimes called Porta Manna or Torre di Mariano after its builder. This tower, of granite, with huge battlements and a smaller tower on top, and the Torre Portixedda, are all that remains of the fortified wall built in 1291. The Portixedda has telephone wires attached to it and stands in a suburban street with nothing like the drama of the other.

There is one other link with Eleonora d'Arborea, and that is the church of Santa Chiara in Via Garibaldi where she is said to have been buried. The church was founded in the first half of the fourteenth century by the Giudice who handed over to Eleonora's father. It has a simple exterior and inside are five gothic arches, a row of animal gargoyles projecting out from the walls and a hideous window behind the altar. Much more imposing is the cathedral which was begun in the early thirteenth century. It stands above the level of the Piazza del Duomo with a gravel courtyard and trees, and you can see that the base of the polygon bell-tower is one of the older sections.

Most of the present church dates from 1733, with a baroque interior, black and white tiled floor, and domes for every chapel. It does have one simple touch, a wooden madonna by Nino Pisano, and she has a severe hairstyle and a robe in blue, gold and red. Next door to the cathedral is the Seminario Tridentino, founded in 1712, and the street is full of gracious old town houses with elegant windows. Very close by is the church of San Francesco, built in the nineteenth century by Gaetano Cima on the site of a gothic church of which a couple of pillars remain. It is small and neat, and seems almost circular with its central dome. At early morning mass are professional people stopping off on their way to work and youngsters en route for school. Four large oil paintings painted by Pietro Cavaro in 1553 which used to hang here, have been removed to the Palazzo Comunale in Piazza del Municipio which also houses a collection by an unknown fifteenth-century Catalan artist.

Oristano is an old-fashioned town with a certain solidity. Many shops are modern, but above is the original façade with stone balconies, columns and rooftop balustrade. The inhabitants are industrious and meticulous – the fishmonger arranges each sardine on his slab with artistic care and the baker fills his window with futuristic and fantastic bread shapes. The mediaeval jamboree, called Sa Sartiglia, marks the end of carnival and the beginning of Lent. It runs for two days, each of which begins with the robing of the Master of Ceremonies, a procession through the streets and then the tilting itself, in which horsemen in Spanish costumes try to push their swords through a suspended silver star – this at full gallop. Any event concerning horses is a popular one on the island and this is more exuberant than most.

6 Province of Oristano

It will be some time before the map-makers catch up with the boundaries that mark the Province of Oristano, which has been formally in existence since the spring of 1975. In size it is very much the smallest of Sardinia's quartet and has been constructed by taking the largest nibble out of Cagliari Province and a lesser bite from Nuoro, giving it a respectable acreage of hinterland and length of coastline. Despite these obvious limitations, the province manages to pack in a goodly variety, though some is of a workaday character.

The lagoons provide both fishing and salt, and coastline agriculture has been expanded by reclaimed land. Inland, the picture is one of sheep and cattle, cork plantations, flourishing oranges and lemons with the mountains never far away. There is nothing spectacular, but it has a gentle restful charm and nowhere is very distant from its provincial capital. It won my heart for its own drink, a special dessert wine, not so much for the taste as because it is marketed under the irresistible label of Sardinian gold!

Taking the main road south from Oristano you have hardly left the suburbs before you reach the enormous Stagno di Santa Giusta with its village of the same name spread out in rather ugly ribbon development along the high road. It is, however, worth pausing, for there is a lovely twelfth-century romanesque church built of blocks of ashlar. The façade is austerely simple, the bell-tower having been rebuilt, and gathering on the steps for mass are the women of the village, uniformly clad in their long pleated skirts. Inside are three naves with marble and granite columns, some of which are romanesque and others actually Roman, brought from Tharros and Othoca.

The route runs across the reclaimed swamp land of the Campidano Minore to reach very quickly the new town of Arborea – a nice touch to keep Eleonora's name alive. It was built in 1928 and has a very neat squared-off appearance with its irrigation channels and canals, eucalyptus trees for windbreaks, straight roads and uninspired houses. Perhaps it does not qualify as a tourist attraction, but it is one of the several between-the-wars developments that are important to Sardinia's agricultural programme. The town marks the southern limit of the Gulf of Oristano, one of the island's quartet of bays.

You can return to the main road through vineyards and Terralba, whose parish church was built on the ruins of a Roman one and was the seat of a bishopric in 1500, and shortly afterwards reach Uras, which like several villages around here has adobe-style clay brick houses. It is a quiet little place, concerned with making carpets and pointing out to visitors its nearby nuraghe Domubeccia, and there is no remembrance or commemoration of a bitter battle in the Middle Ages.

The Aragon Viceroy Carroz marched here in 1470 to meet the Marquis of Oristano to demand submission and tribute to his king. The Marquis had no intention of submitting, and in any case he and Carroz were personal enemies. The whole of the area rushed to the support of the Marquis and the Aragonese were conquered. Much later Uras was once more besieged and defeated the enemy by the simple ruse of pretending there were more in the garrison than the actual pitiful few. They accomplished this by marching troops round and round the church, and the invaders were so bemused by the apparently enormous force that they fled!

South from Uras will bring you soon out of the province, but there is a pleasant detour to be made, inland and eastwards from this village to the mountains. Within minutes of leaving the national highway the centuries peel away. First it is sheep country, then rolling cornfields, with the Monte Arci rising mistily to one side. After passing through the hamlet of Morgongiori the road drops and the ruined castle Barumela is on a hillock just before Ales, where flowers cascade over the balconies and orange and lemon trees are glimpsed in gardens. Its seventeenth-century church seems too big for its boots, but this was the seat of a diocese from 1182 and it remains the centre of the Marmilla region.

Beyond here the road begins to climb, and almond, chestnut and oak trees succeed each other, almost as though each has marked out its own bit of terrain. Cows, sheep, goats and pigs are scattered about the hillside and wandering across the road, and there are innumerable truncated cones of nuraghe. Up here there is an eye-level view of the Giara di Gesturi with its protected wild horses, and the sleepy hill villages with their farmyard smells continue through into Nuoro Province.

Another excursion inland is from Oristano through the valley of the River Tirso, where there is good fishing for trout and carp, and Fordongianus is reached in just over 15 miles. Ptolemy called it Acquae Hypsitanae, but its current name derives from Roman times when it was a colony under Trajan and so named after that man, Forum Trajani. A road the Romans built linked the village with Abbasanta and Oristano and the surrounding wall for which they were also responsible was subsequently destroyed by Vandals and Saracens. Remains from that time include an amphitheatre, baths and catacombs. The romanesque twelfth-century church of San Lussurgiu, just outside, has a fourth-century crypt where relics of the martyr Lussurgiu are said to have been found.

Fordongianus is at a cross-roads, but continue straight on leaving the river bank and climb to the upland villages of Busachi and Ula Tirso, each sited in a 'nest' of nuraghe and giants' tombs. Beyond here turn left on a wiggly gravel road that drops down through the hamlets of Neoneli and Ardauli to the lake of Omodeo, one of Sardinia's largest artificial stretches of water and named after its constructor who dammed the Tirso in 1923. There is no road that actually encircles the lake but its lower end can be crossed by a bridge to enter Ghilarza with its mediaeval buildings, ruined castle, fifteenth-century tower and twelfth-century romanesque church of San Palermo.

Five miles away, either by the main road or by a more picturesque minor track, is Sedilo, which has the most important lead and zinc foundry in Italy, and, more interesting to tourists, is famed for its horsemen and its spectacular Ardia races. In early July it commemorates the victory of the martyr Constantine over a Roman commander with a horseback cavalcade and jousting tournament called S'Ardia di San Constantino. Should you be bitten by a snake in Sardinia, an exceedingly remote prospect as there are said to be no venomous ones at all, then the people of Sedilo have a cure for the bite – a special dance!

From Sedilo retrace the drive to Ghilarza and from thence the couple of miles to Abbasanta where a typical inhabitant is a farmer smoking a pipe, his umbrella slung across his back, ambling along on a donkey. It is a rather sombre agricultural village, no more than a map reference for one of the island's most important Proto-Sard settlements, Nuraghe Losa, and not for the last time all entrances to an historical site are bolted and barred. The basaltic brown blocks of stone, the same as in Abbasanta's houses, rise three storeys high and date from the tenth century B.C., though various sections were added by the Carthaginians and Romans. The truncated central tower, now grass covered, and some of the outlying walls, remain and from the upper terrace, I am told, there is a splendid view of the Altopiano Abbasanta plain.

To return to Oristano from here join the main road south through cork trees and olive groves to Paulilatino and then through scenery where scrub bushes and pasture lands are separated by low-built stone walls. As in Italy, the main roads are littered with advertising signs, and every so often there is a neat enclosure in a field containing a private cemetery sheltered by cypresses.

A third day excursion from the provincial capital heads north-west reaching in a few minutes the romanesque-gothic church of La Maddalena di Rimedio which dates from the second half of the fourteenth century. Two miles further on is a right-hand turn to San Vero Milis, which makes the vernaccia dessert wine with the 'gold' label. The road passes close to the River Mannu to reach Milis, with its orange and lemon groves, plum plantations and reed-mat industry. It has, for such a small place, several ancient churches, including the almost ruined twelfth-century Milis Pizzinu, the Aragonese-gothic parish church, and the thirteenth-century romanesque San Paulo which was later remodelled.

From Milis the road climbs nearly 700 feet in four miles to Bonarcado where the fifth-century sanctuary of Madonna di Bonacattu was enlarged in the mid-thirteenth century. Next door is Santa Maria church consecrated in 1147, expanded a century later to show Saracen influence, and again in the fourteenth century when additions were made to the bell-tower. The road continues rising, crossing the River Sos Molinos to Santa Lussurgiu, whose thin narrow dark houses are built in a crater. Stairways link the different street levels and there is space for little cobbled yards but not for a piazza. The village is enclosed by olive groves and chestnut trees and on Good Friday the inhabitants hold a carnival to their saint.

The scenery round here is naked cork trees with cattle munching beneath them, and the main traffic is animals and farmers wearing corduroys, cloth caps and gum boots with a black poncho slung over the shoulder in case of rain. Their horses have high pommel saddles as in American Westerns and goat-skin panniers carry the food. The road twists up from Santa Lussurgiu with magnificent views over the plain, but before the top there is a right-hand turn to drive down to the little twelfth-century church of San Leonardo de Siete Fuentes where Guelfo, son of Count Ugolino della Gherardesca, was buried in 1292. It is romanesque-gothic and it is in a most charming setting with trees and the little brook which takes its name from the church.

From the top of the pass, at more than 2500 feet, and marked by a chapel, the scenery loses its serenity and becomes much wilder, even sinister on a cold misty day. The trees turn to scrub and the green hills to rocky outcrops atop one of which is perched the Castle of Monte Ferru so cleverly designed that only the big cross on the top catches the eye to indicate its presence. It is only six miles down to Cuglieri which seems very benign after the mountain road. Oranges grow in private gardens, the layout is similar to Santa Lussurgiu as it is also built in a crater, and there is an imposing church overlooking the little town, which was the scene of a sad battle for the Sards when their leader, Amsicora, killed himself after being beaten by the Romans.

It is a ten-mile drive on to the coast and Santa Caterina di Pittinuri with its sentinel tower built as a defence against the Saracens and excellent underwater fishing with an international annual contest for the Cornus Cup. The name is significant, for just south of Santa Caterina is Cornus itself, now in ruins and one of the Roman settlements. Unusually for these conquerors, its history is not well documented. The Sards and Carthaginians who escaped slaughter by the Romans near Cagliari in 215 B.C. fled here, but they were soon afterwards subjugated by their enemies. Cornus was still in existence in the early eleventh century, and no one knows when its final decay and depopulation actually occurred.

The road south from here cuts across the top end of the Sinis peninsula to Cabras, which is not actually on the seashore but looks as though it is with its enormous stagno alongside. This inland lake is full of fish and bird-life and is so shallow that it can be crossed in flimsy punts made of bundles of reeds tied together. The fishermen are said to be able to build a boat in a matter of hours once the raw material has been collected from the nearby marshes. Near the cemetery of the parish church are the remains of a mediaeval castle known as Villa d'Arborea, though when Eleonora lived there they called it the Royal Palace.

From the time of the dissolution of the Giudice nothing is known about the fortress, though the village suffered from raids by pirates and Turks in the early sixteenth century and the French fleet sailed in in 1637. Although Cabras is so close to Oristano it retains its own individuality and it shares with the inhabitants of the provincial capital the resort of Marina di Torre Grande.

From here there is a narrow spit of land with the gulf on one side and the stagno on the other, and it is worth crossing to visit three places which are strung out along the peninsula.

The first is San Salvatore, a simple church with a fascinating history. Reached through a trap door inside, is a pagan temple dating from the fifth century with various Roman deities depicted on the walls – Venus, Cupid and Hercules strangling a lion. Up above, in the much later building, are murals and figures in seventeenth-century Spanish dress, believed to have been painted by prisoners of war interned here. Today San Salvatore comes alive in September when pilgrims from Cabras live here for the festival.

Only a mile or two down the road is another ancient church, that of San Giovanni di Sinis, again a fifth-century part-pagan building to which Christian overtones were added, the newest part dating from the eleventh century. Almost at the tip of the peninsula, with its lighthouse and Cape San Marco, are the ruins of Tharros. Tharros was founded by either the Phoenicians or the Carthaginians, but it was under the latter that it became the agricultural and commercial centre of the Campidano region. Much of the town is submerged beneath the waves and on land many of the stones have been removed by local builders. It is a somewhat sad and desolate spectacle, but perhaps the new provincial authorities will take a hand and bring it back to life so that it can become as beloved a place to Oristano as Nora is to the Cagliarese.

7 Sassari

The folk of Sassari, Sardinia's second largest city, have a well deserved reputation for their ironic, almost satirical view of things. For centuries they were rivals of nearby Alghero, whose inhabitants, in a fit of pique, forced visiting Sassarese to take their swords from their scabbards and leave them at the town gates. Sassari went one better and took revenge by obliging visiting Algherese not only to leave their swords at the city entrance but also to wear two empty scabbards.

Today these sophisticated Sards raise a quizzical eyebrow at such primitive goings-on. Nevertheless they are not above an adverse comment about their former rivals, or about anyone else, because they believe, quite simply, that Sassari is the only city in which to live, so those who are elsewhere by choice deserve scorn. The pretty green city sits atop a plateau well inland, for it began as a mediaeval refugee camp for the fleeting inhabitants of Porto Torres on the coast.

At about the same time, mid-thirteenth century, a 12 year old boy King was elected in Sassari. He was almost immediately slaughtered in a peoples' revolt, an event that might have escaped the historians had not Dante put the leading revolutionary, Michele Zanche, in his Inferno and described him and his Sard friend thus: 'with him's Don Michele Zanche, artists in robbery from Logador; their tongues going clack-clack-clack about Sardinia, kick up a ceaseless bobbery.'

The place today where the tongues go clack-clack-clack is the Piazza d'Italia with its colonnaded cafés. In the centre of the Piazza there is a statue of Vittorio Emanuele, a late nineteenth-century work by Giuseppe

Sartorio. Four tall palms stand guard at each corner, and people sit on the stone benches beneath them to watch the gentle passing scene, enlivened on this evening by youngsters roller-skating, one of whom is using a pair of Alsatian puppies to pull him along. The buildings around the square are not particularly old, but imposing in their way. The Palazzo della Provincia takes up the whole of one side, with a short flight of steps down into the Piazza, and has a balustrade over which people lean. On the opposite side is what was the neo-gothic Palazzo Giordano, its impressive entrance hall now leading into a bank and offices.

A very short street links d'Italia with another square, which used to be called Piazza Castello from the Aragonese castle that once stood there, and is now called Piazza Cavallino de Honestia. The contrast between ancient and modern, old and new buildings, is sharp, and the tall palm trees can be included with the old. The Piazza marks the boundary between modern Sassari and the original walled city, which is full of mediaeval streets. The main artery, that is to say the least narrow street, is the Corso Vittorio Emanuele which is one-way only and which at 6 p.m. is crowded with shoppers and strollers, popping in and out of alleyways, in one of which is an open-air art exhibition.

Some of the houses are fifteenth and sixteenth-century Aragonese, but apart from the mellow renaissance house that used to be the Palazzo del Barone d'Usine and is now the Music Conservatory, situated off the Corso in the Piazza Pasquale Tola, the old-style elegance has been overshadowed by new shop façades. It is very easy to get lost once you have left the Corso, but the whole area is quite small so if something is missed it merely means doubling-back and adding another five minutes to the tour.

One obvious route is down the Via del Duomo leading, of course, to the cathedral of San Nicola. Only the lower part of the bell-tower remains of the thirteenth-century building. The gothic bits, including gargoyles, were added when the archbishopric was transferred here from Porto Torres in 1441, and for years Sassari quarrelled with

Cagliari as to which of them had the right to the title of Primate of Sardinia and Corsica. The church has been restored to its fifteenth-century style, though its best external feature is a magnificent baroque façade with wild flowers clinging tenaciously to an upper ledge. The traffic rushes past almost scraping the steps, but does not permeate the interior, which has a modern rose window above the main altar. San Nicola has two treasures: a marble font from Piedmont with clawed feet; and, in contrast to this ornate piece, a simple madonna of the wood above the altar which, as mass is going on, is luckily lit up and looks beautiful even at a distance.

Around the corner from the cathedral is the Piazza del Comune with one of the largest buildings in the old town, the Palazzo Comunale, originally owned by the Duke of Asinara and heavily restored in 1775. Today it is the town hall, and it has a valuable collection of costume dolls by Eugenio Tavolara. From this Piazza stroll down Via Canopolo to emerge at the public gardens with its pavilion containing a permanent handicraft exhibition. On a festival day the crowd is pressed against the door waiting its turn to get into this splendid showroom of everything Sardinian, from the homely to the exotic.

The island's raw materials, such as dwarf palm, clay, cork, wood, wool, silver, are transformed here into baskets, jars, bridal chests, carpets (up to £750,000 each), filigree jewellery and a centrepiece of a miniature Cavalcata Sarda, the animals in wood and the figures in felt. Another section consists of food and drink, a fine display of most wines and an array of tins of artichokes, tomatoes, fish, pastas and so on. A humble tinned vegetable gets the same close scrutiny from the visitors as do the expensive jewellery and carpets.

Alongside the gardens is the University, which was maintained by the Jesuits after it had been founded in 1588 by Alessio Fontana, secretary to Carlo V. In 1848 the perverse Sassarese put the Jesuits to flight, in the belief that this religious order opposed political liberty. Today's faculties of medicine and veterinary science are famous, and the library has more than 100,000 volumes, including, appropriately, Latin and Spanish manuscripts,

for Sassari also suffered from feuding Genoese, Pisans, Aragonese and neighbouring Giudice. After no less than ten sieges it fell into the hands of Aragon, who in 1420 upgraded its status to that of a city.

Just over a century later the French attacked – and succeeded – though the Sassarese finally managed to expel them, to the delight of the then Spanish King, Carlo V. That would have been quite enough for any city, but in 1529 the plague struck and removed 15,000 of its inhabitants, very likely a major proportion. There was a lull in disaster and warfare for the following 200 years, until Austria came into the picture for a short time – it was that country, incidentally, which introduced tobacco to Sardinia – to be followed by the House of Savoy from 1720.

The best way to tackle the remainder of Sassari's sights is by car, perhaps starting early in the morning at the church of San Francesco, reached from the residential street of the same name, and with a flight of steps to its courtyard and surrounding tamarisks. The church itself, red brick, neo-gothic, is modern and not so much the purpose of the visit as the view from the courtyard over the rooftops to the Plains of Sassari, from which on a clear day, I am told, the sea near Porto Torres is visible.

Not far from here, and easily overlooked with new roads all around, is the Fontana di Rosello tucked below Corso Trinita where some old city walls stand. Leave the flower-seller arranging his carnations and go down a flight of steps through rough grass with trees. At the bottom of the slope is the fountain, a pretty renaissance structure with water spewing out of dolphins. It has the arms of Aragon and Logudoro at the top and the finest aspect are the figures of the Four Seasons, one at each corner.

Drive down Corso Trinita away from the city centre and turn left at the main cross-roads to arrive in Piazza S. Antonio; should you get lost ask the way to the main railway station which is close by. In a cluster in the busy square are a fourteenth-century column with carvings from heroic stories, the Fonte S. Antonio (a very ordinary affair after Rosello) and the church of Sant'Antonio. The latter has a fine façade with elegant stone columns supporting its plain door; inside the style is baroque with an ornate blue and gilt carved altar and enormous oil paintings in every side chapel.

A few hundred yards away, in Via Sant'Apollinare, whose houses are crumbling and unpainted, is the church of the same name, with an unprepossessing exterior. It is worth going in, though, to see the simple black wood fourteenth-century gothic crucifix. There is a distinctly mediaeval smell in these back streets, no less disagreeable than the distinctly twentieth-century diesel smell on the tree-lined Corso Vico nearby. It is this main road you should take to continue the tour of what one might call the outer ring road of Sassari.

The Piazza Santa Maria has a little courtyard with trees, but the church doorway here is not the entrance to the thirteenth-century Santa Maria di Betlemme. Walk round the corner and the length of the building, past a leafy garden providing a buffer against the cars, and you will find the entrance. The exterior, with rows of little arches above the carved main door, is romanesque; inside it is Aragonese-gothic, abounding in mock marble and statuary, and the painted white and gold wooden altars are a good example of local craftsmanship.

From here head for the Viale San Pietro, where the suburban folk take their evening promenade. The little church of San Pietro di Silki is so close to the edge of the city that it overlooks fields. It was built in the thirteenth century, but only the Romanesque bell-tower is original and most of the interior has gothic vaulting. The scene inside, with mass about to start, is as crowded as that in the courtyard, where stalls are open for business.

There is one more church worth a visit, back up the Viale San Pietro to branch right on to Corso Giovannia Maria Angioy and find the Piazza S. Agostino with its sixteenth-century church of the same name, standing next to the military hospital. The interior is high vaulted gothic, though the side chapels alternate between this and romanesque. One of the chapels is dedicated to the Madonna del Buon Cammino, the patron of travellers, and people naturally travel from all over for her festival in August. Almost the only decoration in this simple sombre church is the modern stained glass window behind the altar.

Sassari's Museum G. A. Sanna is really a curtain-raiser for that of Cagliari. It was built by Sanna, a mining engineer, who made the collection, and it is not easy to get in unless you are part of a group, the simple reason being that there are insufficient guards to go round and the authorities fear pilfering if people wander about by themselves. Unluckily, too, there was no catalogue in any language on my visit, though each room is beautifully documented and illustrated in Italian. What the museum does is to give you an idea of the way of life of the nuraghic people – their funeral urns, implements, shell jewellery, intricate decoration on bowls, fertility stones, carved animal heads, with a small collection of the famous bronze statuettes.

The Roman objects are perhaps more familiar, and they include jewellery that is solid both in shape and substance (gold), and a fine black and white mosaic from Porto Torres. The ethnographical section contains most of the items you will already have seen or be about to see on the island, except that the costumes and jewellery are marginally older. Certainly the bread designs – birds, leaves, flowers and so on – are in the best bakeries, as are the bridal chests in private homes.

But the real charm of this part of the museum is the discovery that today's Sardinian craftsmen, whether they are baking bread, weaving carpets, making costumes or furniture or jewellery, have followed the old designs. This means that the exhibits do not appear as museum pieces but rather as an opportunity for a close inspection of things Sardinian.

8   Province of Sassari

The appeal of the Province of Sassari is that whatever your interest, save for the highest mountains, you will find it here. It comprises a large clean slice from the top of the map, with a very large portion of coastline and an off-shore archipelago. But this geographical outline says nothing about a series of regions so diverse in style, history and people that they prove again that the independent Sard character is sub-divided into dozens of independent characters.

Even the animals seem to have been influenced by their masters' wish to be different! For there is a strange albino donkey that has evolved from a wild ass and lives, as it has always done, on one tiny island only. In much the same way the folk of Alghero, speaking Catalan, regard themselves as a race apart from the other Sards, although they are on the mainland and only half an hour's drive from Sassari. A different sort of enclave is the development of the Costa Smeralda, a luxury play-ground in the north-east which was once the poorest region on the island. The inhabitants migrated in search of work and are now returning to find home has become an alien place peopled by foreigners but nonetheless providing jobs.

Religion and paganism exist side by side quite natural-ly here. Indeed many of those involved in the Second World War and the allied bombing owe their survival, they believe, to a miracle, and show their appreciation in a remarkable way. Many of their saints date from the times of Roman persecution and are suitably revered. Paganism is an excuse for a grand bonfire and the burning of the effigy of King Carnival.

If history is your particular interest, then you can trace its development in this province, beginning with the Proto-Sards, continuing through the Middle Ages when it was the habit of various invaders to change the name of the place they conquered, up to the nineteenth century and two outstanding figures, Britain's Nelson and Italy's Garibaldi, both of whom were around the group of islands that sits in the straits separating Sardinia from Corsica.

The provincial capital makes a handy base from which to explore much of the province, and perhaps the most appropriate place to start is Porto Torres, for it was from here that the inhabitants fled inland to found the then little village of Sassari. They left a flourishing port, in fact Turris Libissonis, as the Romans called it, was as important to the north of the island as Karalis (Cagliari) was to the south. Following the decline of that Empire, however, it fell victim to the usual squabbles between Pisa and Genoa, and when the latter sacked it for the last time in 1166, most of the natives retreated. Oddly, though, it was not until much later that their Giudice and Archbishop made the 12-mile journey to follow them to what is now the provincial capital.

Now, in the twentieth century, Porto Torres has been revitalised and, with its ferry services to Genoa, Livorno and Civitavecchia, is a bustling place. The burgeoning oil refineries and factories on the outskirts of town almost obscure the fine Roman bridge over the River Turritano whose seven arches decrease in size to accommodate the different height of either bank. It is still the traveller's entry to the town, though a modern bridge takes the departing traffic and provides the best view of the earlier construction. There is another Roman heritage which is also easy to miss, for it is almost entirely engulfed by the railway station and sidings. But slowing down to cross the tracks you will see an unkempt Roman ruin containing baths, columns, bits of mosaics and the remains of the Barbarian's Palace.

The origins of the latter are not entirely clear, but it was said to have started life as a temple dedicated to the

Goddess of Fortune, though its name derives from the fact that it was the palace of a Roman governor called Barbarus. Later it was taken over by the Giudice and renamed Palazzo di Torres, and Constantino died there in 1127. It has reverted to its Roman name because Barbarus was in power at the martyrdom of San Gavino, one of the major saints among the countless claimed by Sardinia, and rather more authenticated than some. It seems Gavino, a Roman commander during the reign of Emperor Diocletian, was converted by two condemned Christians, Protus and Januarius, and suffered the same fate, all three being beheaded in A.D. 300.

What happened to their bodies remained a mystery for more than a thousand years, but meanwhile the Giudice of Torres, or the Pisans, depending upon which history book you support, in the eleventh century built the basilica of San Gavino and by a lucky chance chose a hill then quite distant from the port so that it remains in splendid isolation. The Lombards expanded the cathedral and it is said to be the largest mediaeval church in Sardinia, though it has much to offer as well as size. Its setting is a Mediterranean version of an English cathedral close, a courtyard on each side of the basilica ringed by tiny dilapidated cottages with outside staircases to the first floors. Old women in black are filling water containers from a pump in the middle of one courtyard and children are playing a complicated game with sticks.

The exterior of San Gavino has the appearance of a fortress, deliberately, as it was designed to withstand the attacks of the Corsairs, though not always successfully. The stone has mellowed over the centuries to a warm yellow and the high double row of archers' slits, which act as windows, no longer look menacing. There are three doors, built later than the church, two of them fifteenth-century Catalan-gothic and the other rebuilt from a romanesque door. All are firmly locked and consultations with the water-carriers reveal that churches cannot be visited between the hours of noon and 4.30 p.m.

A second visit at the appointed time is half successful, in that the church itself is open. Birds are living in the high wooden rafters and the three naves are separated by slender columns and pillars of differing kinds, but mainly Doric and Corinthian, which were dug up around the neighbourhood and sensibly used as building material. In 1927, a seventh-century Byzantine panel telling how the Sards were victorious over the Longobards was found in the ruins of a little church near the railway station and it now has a place in San Gavino. The bolted crypt of the basilica proves impenetrable. The priest is not in his house; the nun in the church has no idea; half a dozen small boys comb all available places in search of the man with the key, to no avail.

But I am assured that it does contain three Roman sarcophagi with the relics of Gavino, Protus and Januarius and legend has it that the Giudice of Torres put them there. In 1614 the bones were dug up and one Sard, writing a couple of centuries later, insists that the exhumation was attended by miracle cures, celestial music and a scented smell from the tombs, thus proving that the relics were really those of the saints. San Gavino, after such a history, naturally has his own feast day, when on May 4 the people of Porto Torres have a procession from the basilica to the chapel of San Gavino a Mare, perched on a clifftop. For an added romantic touch, the caves in these particular cliffs were once inhabited by hermits.

It is only 20 or so miles from here to the north-west tip of Sardinia through not very interesting scenery, until you reach Stintino, settled at the end of the nineteenth century by a group of fishermen and shepherds who used to live on the nearby island of Asinara. The village has a double cove to take its fishing fleet and an increasing number of smart yachts and motor boats. As well as tunny fishing, the mattanza here being on a similar scale to that of the island of San Pietro, there are lobster pots specially designed to return unharmed to the sea the small and young specimens.

Beyond the village begins an expensive development of scattered and discreet villas whose owners have one of the most beautiful beaches on the island, that of La Pelosa, with white sand and turquoise water. At land's end is

Cape Falcone, where underwater fishing contests take place, and on top of the hill, covered with scrub to soften the rocks, is the Torre Falcone, put up by the Spaniards who, once they had conquered Sardinia seemed to have a fixation about further invasions. Sitting squatly between the Cape and the island of Asinara is the baby Isola Piana, and even this has its protective Torre Pelosa.

Asinara, ten miles long and four miles wide, which the Romans called Sinuaria because of its jagged coastline, looks like four separate islands instead of one. Its name is derived from its wild asses who in their turn produced an albino donkey which survives today. There was a naval engagement on its shores in the early fifteenth century, in which the Sicilians beat the Genoese, and the coral fishery later established by the Sassarese, was disturbed by attacks from African pirates. In 1638 French Corsairs took possession and used it as a raiding base for ships passing by or trading with Porto Torres.

The island used to belong to the Duke of Vallombrosa whose forefathers bought it in 1775 from Vittorio Amadeo III. It is connected to the mainland by a thrice weekly boat service from Porto Torres carrying goods but rarely passengers, for Asinara has been taken over by the Italian Government and used first as an international sanitary station for quarantine and now as an agricultural penal colony. The highest point, at 1200 feet, has, in the circumstances, a poignant ring, for it is called Punta della Scomunica (Excommunication Point). The prisoners, though, built the church at Stintino for the dispossessed islanders.

To follow the Spanish theme to its headquarters, as it were, you must go to Alghero, which is around 40 miles south of the Stintino peninsula, but is best reached from Porto Torres via a side road, or direct from Sassari on the fast highway. Though the written Spanish language, apart from a few poets, has virtually disappeared, the people speak Catalan and remain sturdily pro-Spanish, as they have done for 600 years. There is almost a deliberate policy not to have contacts with other Sards and my guide says emphatically: 'We are an island on an island.'

Considering the events that led to the Spanish domination here, their pride seems misplaced to the visitor. The town had been founded and fortified by the Doria family and they held it for 250 years apart from a brief spell of Pisan occupation in 1283. A family quarrel resulted in some Dorias selling their rights and possessions to Pedro IV, King of Aragon, who took advantage of the family split to further his own ends. He sent in a substantial naval and military force in 1353 and though the opposing Genoese force was larger they were beaten, losing more than half their fleet as well as a casualty list of 3000 prisoners and 8000 dead.

But the moment the victorious Spanish admiral left, the Algherese turned against and murdered their new rulers. So Pedro IV tried again the following year, this time with an armada of 90 ships and well over 10,000 troops. Even so, the besieged townspeople, with only 700 men, held out for four months, and when Pedro heard that the Giudice of Arborea was coming to the rescue with an even larger force than his own he entered into terms with Alghero. The apparently humane conditions permitted the Dorias and the Genoese to leave the town, allowed them to keep their possessions in other parts of the island and a few years later, in 1360, Pedro made the land around Alghero a gift to its citizens. The Giudice of Arborea and the Genoese made two abortive and ill-designed attempts to recapture the town, and the second resulted in the death of every one of the attackers.

In 1391 the Aragon King struck with his major plan, to make Alghero a Spanish base, his first step being to exile all the inhabitants to Villanova and replace them with a colony of Catalans. Some Sards were allowed to work in the town, but they had to withdraw before sunset. Laws were passed stating that at the sound of a trumpet call all Sards must leave immediately, and in any case no more than ten at a time could enter Alghero. The new colony was given special privileges to ensure its continued safety and prosperity. There were special coral fishing limits to be used only by boats of Alghero; only Catalans were allowed to trade and each trader was permitted to sell a large quantity of wheat without paying any duty provided he had a cross-bow and 100 arrows

and promised to practice, by shooting half a dozen
arrows every Sunday.

While part of the Spanish ramparts were destroyed at
the beginning of this century, the walled city still has
seven towers and, by coincidence, seven churches. The
best place to start is on top of the walls where you can
admire the superb views of harbour, port and sea. The
tall thin houses now extend above the walls, and most
doors and windows remain open to give passing pedestrians a cosy insight into family breakfasts.

There is only one ground-level entrance to the city on
the harbour side, the Porto a Mare with a barometer in
the archway so that fishermen can judge the weather;
most pay their respects to the madonna in a little niche
on the opposite wall. Inside the doorway is the Piazza
Civica with the sailors' snooker club next door to the
Palazzo d'Albis where Carlo V, King of Spain, stopped
off for a few days in 1541, on his way to Algiers with an
expedition. He is supposed to have addressed the populace from a now bricked-up first-floor window in the
palace, exhorting them to courtly behaviour to combat the
rowdiness of the troops he brought with him – a nice line
in mediaeval pep talk.

The Piazza is protected by the Maddalena bastion, the
last of the fortifications to be built and because of its
open back a good one in which to see how the ramparts
were continually altered and how the interior walls were
attached to the outside ones. They were built sloping out-
wards to resist attacking guns, but in at least one addition there was an unfortunate structural error so that the
latest defence point successfully blocked off the firing line
of the original, thus certainly not killing two birds with
one stone. Maddalena tower is dedicated to Garibaldi
who in 1855 arrived here in a boat hired by several
Algherese families to escape a cholera epidemic.

Of the remaining towers, only two have historical tales
to tell. Torre dello Sperone, in Piazza Sulis, built in the
sixteenth century, is now crowded by modern buildings,
and its most celebrated prisoner was Vincenzo Sulis, who
remained here for 30 years following his part in an uprising at Cagliari in the early nineteenth century. The

Torre di Porta Terra, sometimes called the Torre degle Ebrei, in Via Sassari, was closed every night until 1848, the guards making the traditional cry of 'whoever is inside, stays inside.' On this particular morning 'whoever is inside' includes travelling salesmen, their car roof-racks piled high, hooting their way through the narrow streets and offering either toilet rolls or plastic rubbish bags, presumably on a bulk-buy basis.

The most important ecclesiastical building is the cathedral, which was built in the sixteenth century at about the same time Alghero was created a diocese on the consolidation of the three minor bishoprics of Ottana, Castro and Bisarcio. Its foundation, in 1510, came just seven years after Alghero was promoted in rank from town to city, but it has been much altered over the years, including a complete reconstruction during the eighteenth and nineteenth centuries. The sixteenth-century Aragonese-gothic bell-tower, with its gargoyles, and the gothic back door are the best external features. Inside are three lofty naves separated by alternating pillars and columns, an octagonal dome, and a baroque pulpit and altar behind which is a nineteenth century monument to Maurice, Duke of Savoy, a neo-classic marble study of women and nymphs. The presbytery has a splendid portrait gallery of all the bishops of Alghero.

In Piazza Ginnasio is the seventeenth-century baroque church of San Michele, with black and white altar and enormous square pillars which are being thoroughly dusted with a Cinderella-broom by a Jesuit. The church of San Francesco, in Via Carlo Alberto, largely rebuilt in the eighteenth century, has a tranquil cloister and an attractive bell-tower. The new churches, with their multi-coloured domes in geometric criss-cross patterns, reveal a continuing Spanish influence. There are only a couple of non-religious buildings of merit in the old city, one being the Casa Doria, which has nothing whatever to do with the family of that name, but is a gracious sixteenth-century renaissance house; and the Palazzo Comunale, which has the historical archives of the town, including autographs of King Carlo.

Outside the walls, by the harbour, is the visible

evidence of Alghero's name, from the Latin for seaweed, though my guide in true Sard fashion insists that it is not exactly that, but a first cousin of the weed that is so prevalent in the area. In the shelter of the ramparts the cafés and stalls are setting up for the day's business, a large private yacht is just arriving and the first cruise is setting off for the famous grottoes nearby. Men in teams of six are unloading the sardines from the fishing smacks in concentrated silence, first raking them out of a tank on each boat using a basket sieve, then packing them into shallow boxes to be loaded on to the waiting lorry.

South of the harbour and town is a string of beach hotels, including a splendid Walt Disney-style castle on the sea-front that used to be the holiday home of the King of Italy. New holiday developments are extending down the coast. The countryside around Alghero is pleasant, and tiny shrines on the roofs of houses underline the fact that this was monastery-owned land. One of the most charming excursions is but five miles on a gravel road through olive plantations to the Sanctuary of Valverde, nestling beneath a hill.

Legend says a statue of the madonna was mysteriously found here, and when it was placed in the cathedral it equally mysteriously disappeared from there to re-emerge back at Green Valley. Bowing to the madonna's will, the present chapel was built and throughout April and May pilgrims visit to thank the madonna for her intervention. More interesting yet, the grateful worshippers leave behind a pictorial record of how she saved them. The side altars are cluttered with dramatic scenes, such as a ship breaking up in a storm, a car crash, a war casualty, a recovery from illness, and so on, often with a photograph of the happy survivor. The artistic efforts may not be expert, but the total effect is magnificent.

North of Alghero, past the town beach of San Giovanni there is a camping site beneath the trees and a flat plain where nuraghe are scattered about in the same profusion as the pill-boxes built to repel the British during the Second World War. Indeed a friend remarked that the two constructions, both squat and covered in grass and flowers, were beginning to look like each other! The road passes through the town of Fertilia, another of Mussolini's efforts founded in 1936 on reclaimed land, before it reaches the spectacular Porto Conte, which the Romans romantically called Portus Nimpharum, or Nymphs' Bay.

It is said to be the widest natural harbour in the Mediterranean, and at its entrance stands the fifteenth-century Torre Nuova. There used to be a port-able ladder to reach the door at first-floor level, which the guards within prudently pulled up behind them when they were on watch. Next to the tower, by way of con-trast, is a modern luxury hotel which in place of a non-existent beach has provided an indoor-outdoor pool with a plastic partition separating the two, but enabling swim-mers to make the transfer in one breathless stroke. It is certainly needed on this windy point, where the olive trees in the garden have piles of stones at their base to prevent them blowing over.

On the other headland of the bay, via a nerve-racking clifftop road, is Cape Caccia and one of Sardinia's most famous grottoes, the Grotta di Nettuno. This you can visit by boat from Alghero or, if the sea is too rough and you have made the drive to the Cape, via the Escala del Cabriol which has some 650 steps down the cliff-face, just about one step for every foot lost in height.

To complete Alghero's history, drive southwards on a sharply rising inland road to Villanova Monteleone, the town to which the Algherese were exiled. The Aragonese-gothic church was altered in 1789 and a mile or so out-side the town is the Benedictine sanctuary of Nostra Signora d'Interrios. As well as the original refugees, the population here was augmented by others from nearby Monteleone Rocca Doria, perched on an isolated lime-stone hill, who were fleeing from their own town captured by tribesmen from Bosa. Unlike the Villanova folk, whose speciality is making table linen with stylised birds and geometrical designs, the Rocca Doria inhabitants are farmers and spend a large part of their lives in the sad-dle, riding on horses of Arab descent.

From here it is about ten miles further on to Pozzomaggiore and you can cut east to rejoin the fast highway, first pausing at the twelfth-century church of

San Nicolo di Trullas, and then at Bonorva, which has two items of historical interest in the neighbourhood. The first is the Domus de Janus Sant'Andrea Priu, with 20 interconnecting tombs; the second is a spot called Aidu de Turdu where the defeat of the Aragonese lieutenant-general by the Dorias took place in 1347. The beaten forces hid themselves in the woods around Bonorva and, so the story goes, the commander was so overcome with humiliation, not to speak of the more practical matters of food and water, that he died there.

Sassari is only an hour's drive from here, but there are a couple of worthwhile detours to be made, to visit another famous nuraghe, that of Sant'Antine, excavated in 1934, which until Su Nuraxi was uncovered had the number one place in Sardinia. It is also known as Nuraghe Major because the plain on which it stands is littered with lesser examples. Nearby, almost within walking distance of each other, are a cluster of other sights. Turning left off the main road at Nostra Signora de Cabu Abbas, it is four miles to Thiesi with its terraced hillsides and nearby Lake Bidighinzu and from there a very short step to Borutta where a side road leads to San Pietro di Sorres, once the cathedral of the diocese of the same name. The church is thirteenth-century Pisan-romanesque and contains the tomb of a bishop, the ruins of whose palace are nearby.

Up the road, among cherry orchards and barley fields, is Bonnanaro where a celebrated Sard poet, Francesco Carboni, was born in 1746. He was educated at the university of Sassari and became a member of the Jesuit College until its dissolution, when he moved to Cagliari with the splendid appointment of Professor of Eloquence. Unfortunately, Carboni's political views seemed to have clashed with authority and he returned to Italy for a while before returning to live until his death in 1817, in the tiny hamlet of Bessude, almost next door to Bonnanaro.

Alghero was not the only place in the Province of Sassari that the Spaniards found important. To reach their second stronghold makes a pleasant day excursion, for the road through the region of Anglona is thoughtfully circular and though twisty in some sections the mileage is not daunting. Head first north-east towards the coast and the final destination of Castel Sardo. Tamarisk trees on both sides of the road join together to form a tunnel and the scenery is cornfields, tall hedgerows and little hillocks before reaching the neighbouring villages of Sorso and Sennori, whose villages make the famous dwarf-palm leaf baskets. In addition, Sorso has the remains of Roman villas and baths and an eleventh-century Pisan church called San Michele di Plaiano.

Its marina is three miles away on the coast road, which goes west to Porto Torres and east past endless beaches until a couple of miles before Castel Sardo. Here a side road leads to the church of Nostra Signora de Tergu, built in 1121 on the site of a Roman temple which itself was built on the site of a Proto-Sard temple. The façade is all that remains of the twelfth-century Pisan building and the church, like so many in Sardinia, was once part of a Benedictine monastery.

Castel Sardo is visible long before you reach it, for it is entirely dominated by the castle which perches on top of a small promontory. When the Dorias built it in 1102 they called it Castel Genovese, but though they originally swore allegiance to the King of Aragon, their loyalty proved fickle – largely because of family feuds. After various hostile attacks and a siege in 1448 the Aragonese captured it and Alfonso V changed its name to Castel Aragonese, as well as partly demolishing the fortress. Carlo V of Spain regarded the town with the same importance as Alghero and in 1511 extended similar privileges and immunities to it. The Dorias, backed up by 4000 French troops, failed in an attempt to regain possession in 1527 and 250 years later, in 1767, the town got its third and final name, Castel Sardo, from Carlo Emanuele III.

The predominantly grey houses are clustered below the castle and there is a tiny beach with people sunning themselves on the rocks and an impromptu football game on a sandy mini-pitch. The car is ditched after the first steep section of road at a viewpoint which shows the coastline with its white beach fringe. Over the parapet wall you look down on tiny roof gardens and crammed into a ridiculously small space are broad beans, dwarf palm and bright yellow marguerites. Cars are allowed up here, but they prove a bit of a nuisance to pedestrians, who have to leap into shops to avoid them.

Artigianato Sardo is the generic name for all shops selling handicrafts and this is the only place on the island where the tourist seems to provide the main livelihood of the inhabitants. For a start, it is the one town where the souvenir shops in Via Marmora are all open at 3 p.m., disregarding the usual Sard custom of a long siesta until 5 p.m. The most popular items for sale are those made of dwarf palm, for which Castel Sardo is famous, as it is for its lobsters, though sadly for holidaymakers almost all the latter are exported to Marseilles.

Inside the castle gates is a maze of reconstruction and different styles, with a modern brick staircase up to the battlements where children are playing. There is one original room, open to the sky, with romanesque arches and pillars, but the rest of the castle is decidedly reproduction, badly done, and alas the walls are daubed with graffiti. The view, though, is original, over the Gulf of Asinara on one side and to the mountains of Gallura on the other. The walk back is down cobbled stone steps, to find that some of the houses have fine polished wood doors with brass knockers while others are falling into a sad state of dilapidation.

The cathedral is notable for its eighteenth-century carved wooden altars and choir-stalls and for a gilt and wood pulpit covered with cherubs. In search of its masterpiece, a madonna and child with angels painted by an unknown artist, I unlock a door in one of the chapels and discover a bunch of rabbits living cheerfully at the bottom of a flight of steps, complete with hutch and lettuce. The surprise is almost as great as the madonna herself, who takes up the whole of one side chapel and is quite beautiful.

From Castel Sardo the main road inland runs up the valley a few miles to Elephant Rock, so called because it looks like this animal with its trunk stretching out over the road and its backside covered in yellow lichen. It is

facing the wrong way for the view over the lush green plain to the sea and its trachytic stone interior is full of small chambers with barely discernible decorations, but it is fun to clamber about as young visitors do. The road continues rising to Sedini, some of whose houses are actually constructed from rock faces while others use one natural rock wall as a backing. The church of San'Andrea has an Aragonese-gothic façade of 1517 and just out of the village is the ruined fifteenth-century San Nicola di Silanis, the rest of the Benedictine abbey buildings having entirely disappeared.

Just beyond Bulzi the road crosses the River Silanis and downstream is the thirteenth-century San Pietro di Simbranos o d'Immagini, standing serenely in a meadow with its black and white façade but no bell-tower. Shortly afterwards are cross-roads; turn right for the return trip to Sassari and the first little village is Laerru, built on the slopes of a landslide. Some petrified trees are around if you can find them, as well as the nearby Grotta de su Coloru, which requires something of an expedition to reach.

Martis is nothing more than a road junction, and you climb steadily up to Nulvi, at about 1500 feet, which sits at the foot of Monte San Lorenzo among vineyards. It keeps alive old traditions including wailing for the dead, performs a cycle of plays in Holy Week and at its annual festival in August carries giant candles, as does Sassari at a similar event. The folk not working in the vineyards are busy at looms weaving carpets and wall-hangings. The road and railway criss-cross each other for the next 12 miles to Osilo, where is woven the coarse woollen cloth used for the national costumes. They also make a rosé wine here which is said to have inspired a poet to compose a sonnet to it, quite a recommendation, and worth a final stop on the excursion.

For the rest of the province, pack a suitcase and leave Sassari, either by the speedy dual-carriageway or, much more fun, by the aptly named Scala di Giocca (the spiral staircase). You travel down and round the steep bends, joining the main road below for only four miles before branching left to the tall bell-tower of Santa Trinita di

Saccargia which reaches up into the sky. The abbey stands on a fertile plain, but when the isolated monks first began to cultivate the land around, it was not so benign and they lived for part of the year over the valley at Codrongianos to escape malaria. The legend that led to the building of Santa Trinita is a charming one.

The Giudice of Logudoro and his wife were on their way north to Porto Torres to pray to San Gavino for a child. They spent the night here and by a divine revelation the lady learnt that she was already pregnant, so the pilgrimage was no longer necessary. In gratitude the Giudice paid for the building of the abbey, which is a spectacular example of twelfth-century Pisan-romanesque architecture. Its striking horizontal striped façade is of white limestone and black basalt which was added some 60 years after the foundation of the church in 1116, and although some of the abbey buildings have been transformed into farms, while others are in ruins, much of the basic structure remains.

You step down into the porch with its elegant archways, then up the three steps to enter the church. Space is emphasized by the absence of any columns and the slit windows are almost at the wooden ceiling level. The pulpit is white wood with gold decoration and reached by a discreet door around the corner, and the central of the three semi-circular apses contains the abbey's most impressive internal feature. These are thirteenth-century frescoes and form a beautiful backcloth to the simple altar. Stacked to one side of the nave are pieces of broken column which match up with those in the porch and part of the cloisters. Fig trees now grow in the unruly garden and a persistent cuckoo and cowbells add to the tranquil atmosphere.

From here the road goes through lush countryside with green hillocks and only two miles from Santa Trinita are two more churches, both on the outskirts of Ploaghe, a town built on the site of the pre-Carthaginian village of Plorace, and itself a bishopric in the Middle Ages. Nearby Sant'Antonio was built in the thirteenth century by monks from Vallombrosa, and the twelfth-century Pisan-romanesque San Michele di Salvenero has lost most of its bell-tower but contains a fifteenth-century statue of St Michael. Ardara, six miles up the road, was equally important in the Middle Ages, as the seat of the judiciary of Torres as well as being the capital of Logudoro.

Its church of Santa Maria del Regno was meant to be the chapel of the nearby twelfth-century castle; and its altar contains the consecration stone of 1170 as well as an ornate tableau composed of 30 panels on a gold background, the work of two sixteenth-century artists. Santa Maria was built by the sister of another Sard heroine, like Eleonora d'Arborea. This Giudice led the troops, in her brother's absence, to defeat the usurper of the Giudice of Gallura whom she imprisoned in her castle. The castle was captured from the Dorias by the Aragonese in 1335 and 20 years later was sold to the Giudice of Arborea. This did not, however, prevent the Kings of Aragon from claiming it in the usual ding-dong battles, and it was probably quite relieved to fall into desertion and decay in the fifteenth century.

There is yet one more church to be seen on this stretch of road, that of Sant'Antioco di Bisarcio, originally built in 1090 and reconstructed in 1170 when the bell-tower was added. It subsequently became the cathedral of the diocese that bore its name and included 15 parishes as well as Ozieri in its limits until 1503. The latter town can be reached from Bisarcio by a tranquil lane where farmers riding horses or donkeys herd sheep up the road; where cows graze in the hedgerows instead of in the fields; and where an occasional industrious man scythes the flowering verges for cattle fodder.

Ozieri is a pretty hill town whose almond blossom streets wind up and down and where most of the outlying population have come for the market. There is the fountain Grisoni, a promenade and viewpoint from the Passeggiata di San Michele, and the sixteenth-century cathedral whose Aragonese-gothic façade was destroyed in the nineteenth-century reconstruction. Inside, though, are several treasures: a painting of the Last Supper by Giovanni Marghinotti who lived in the first half of the nineteenth century; a sixteenth-century silver gothic cross; and, best of all, the Madonna di Loreto by a sixteenth-century Sassarese painter who is now known as the Maestro d'Ozieri.

From here the road continues east through hill villages where it is the custom to pull a chair out of doors and sit in the street, in the absence of any pavements. In Pattada, a village that makes horn knife handles, decorated gourds and wrought ironwork, a blacksmith is working in the main street. Shortly afterwards the road turns sharply south and begins the long haul downwards. The Goceano range of mountains form a fine backcloth through Bultei to Bono, which at one stage was captured by Aragon forces and yielded a great deal of booty to the victors, and which, much later was the birthplace of Giovanni Maria Angioy, an aristocrat who took the people's part and led an anti-feudal revolt in the eighteenth century.

The road by-passes Burgos, with its 1127 Castle of Goceano where Adelasia of Torres was imprisoned by her husband Enzo, King of Sardinia, and finally reaches the River Tirso where there is a fine Roman bridge and a main road that will take you almost immediately out of Sassari province and into that of Nuoro. So double-back to Pattada and take a side road that meanders north to Oschiri which has nearby, one of Sardinia's largest artificial lakes, the Coghinas, formed in 1926 to supply hydro-electric power. Take the route that passes the eastern end of the lake and keeps the Limbara mountain-range in view, to reach Tempio Pausania, capital of the region of Gallura.

In February the folk here hold a festival which is entirely pagan, called Corsi Mascherati, and celebrates the death of King Carnival. There are bonfires and floats and the offering of corn fritters and their famous white wine to the public. For the rest of the year they are an industrious community, possibly because they live healthily and coolly at over 1500 feet, and are surrounded by natural resources to give them diverse livings. There is the cork industry, the fibrous tissues that come away with the bark being used to dye wool and goat hair. There are the abundant rivers that in the early days supplied water to the Costa Smeralda and now help along the tourist trade with trout fishing. Above all, there is the thermal water which comes out of Fonte Renaggiu a mile out of town.

It is difficult for a visitor to get near the source, so keen are the locals to collect it as it spews out of the wall unromantically into a horse trough. Should you forget to bring your own container, anything up to a 20-litre plastic jerrycan is on sale, though there is supposed to be a ban on filling the larger receptacles during the daytime. While they wait their turn, the inhabitants sit on benches among the trees in a parklike setting and chat things over.

Back in Tempio centre, the atmosphere is of a pleasant English county town, where people have plenty of time for mid-morning coffee and ice-cream in the Via Roma, where those at the cafés pull their feet in sharply when cars pass on a one-way traffic system which though quite impenetrable to the visitor is entirely justified. Tired of catching a glimpse of where you want to be, but ever failing to reach it, park out of the narrow streets then wander back.

In Piazza San Pietro is the fifteenth-century Aragonese-romanesque cathedral of the same name. It was restored in the nineteenth century but the carved wooden door and steeple are original. The interior is not very interesting, with the exception of a fine fifteenth-century painting in a side chapel and the dark carved wood choir-stalls. On the opposite side of the Piazza is the Oratory with an elegant romanesque façade, a roof that curves up to enfold the bell in the middle and a plain scruffy door, locked.

Many of the houses in Tempio are eighteenth-century, either plain grey granite or prettied up in pinks, yellows and oranges, their balconies a splash of geraniums. The main square is aptly called Piazza Gallura after the region, and though it is a pity that cars are allowed to form a semi-circular parking ring, it is still a handsome piazza with the town hall taking up the whole of one side.

Four miles from Tempio is Aggius, in an area which looks as though a giant has pettishly emptied his playbox of rocks and thrown them carelessly about. The neat cork trees with their chocolate-brown naked lower trunks and their precise lean to one side away from the prevailing wind, make a pleasant contrast to the wilder rockier scenery that alternates with them. Aggius has two claims to fame: it witnessed a particularly vehement feud even by Sardinian standards, between two families, that left only six survivors and killed 72; and, much nicer, it has a famous choir which has taken part in the Welsh eisteddfod.

Return to Tempio from here to continue eastwards to Calangianus with its cork school, and then to join the main highway to Olbia, which, like Castel Sardo, has had several names over the centuries but, uniquely, has reverted to its first one, meaning happy. No one knows for sure when it was founded, but some say as early as the fourth century B.C. by the Carthaginians, followed a couple of centuries later by the Phoenicians. In 259 B.C. comes the first written evidence, by the Romans, when their commander Lucius Cornelius Scipio attacked both Corsica and Sardinia and defeated the Carthaginian general Hanno.

Scipio not only expelled the enemy, he also took as prisoners back to Rome thousands of Sards. As the nearest port to the mouth of the Tiber, Olbia thrived until about the mid-fifth century A.D., when it was destroyed. By 893 it had been rebuilt, become a bishopric and gained a new name, Civita. The Pisans took over in 1198 and the town was again destroyed in the ensuing battles with the Genoese. Its reconstruction produced yet another name, Terranova, which was to stick for well over 700 years, though the new title made no difference to the continuing warfare and raids. The Pisans and the Genoese went on fighting, the Barbary Corsairs raided three times and in 1553 the French and Turkish fleets got into the act with the worst battle yet.

Fresh from their successes in Corsica, and vehemently opposed to the Spanish crown and Carlo V, the Turkish admiral Dragute not only sacked and burned the town, but seized a large portion of the population while it was at mass and carried it off from the church in chains.

Almost the only good thing that happened throughout Olbia's history the English were responsible for. Their fleet was cruising off Sardinia in 1711 to intercept the Spaniards, when Admiral Norris heard that the town had been seized by Count de Castiglione. He landed 1000 men and after a crisp battle near the Church of San Simplicio the Spanish count surrendered.

The next lot of foreigners to land were anything but successful. A small force of Austrians arrived in 1717, having been led to believe that the inhabitants had revolted against Philip of Spain and were now on their side. The wily townsfolk went along with the scheme and duped the enemy by lending them a priest to guide them to Alghero. The Austrians had not gone very far on their journey when they were ambushed by a tiny force of 80 men and returned to Terranova as prisoners. Not until 1939 did Terranova become Olbia, by which time its port and communications were fast developing.

Today it must have the worst traffic-jam problem on the island, with cars heading out on the causeway to Isola Bianca, the ferry terminus for Genoa, Civitavecchia and Arbatax; or to the harbour area in a huge almost landlocked bay, the watery cemetery of Phoenician, Carthaginian and Roman ships; or to the new airport where a couple of jets have just decanted a convention of American car dealers on their way to the Costa Smeralda.

Away from all this bustle is one of the finest churches in Sardinia, that of San Simplicio outside which stall-holders are setting up for the forthcoming Saint's feast day. The eleventh-century church is light grey and there are rows of arches down both sides. Inside a group of children are learning their catechism. The three naves are separated by alternating pillars and columns in the same grey, and the only light is from the high-up slit windows. The effect is heightened, as in other churches, by the wooden ceiling, and behind the altar are some very faded thirteenth-century frescoes.

South of Olbia the coast road passes holiday development increasingly taking advantage of the lagoons and inlets that make up the shoreline. At Porto S. Paulo, for instance, the original village is on the main road and the smart resort is at the water's edge overlooking a tremendous hunk of granite called Tavolara island, with a baby brother nearby, the island of Molara, sometimes known as Buccinaria from the crustaceans that cling to its rocks.

Tavolara gets its name from its impressive flat top and there is a charming tale of a shepherd who lived with his wife and considered himself – he was, incidentally, the only human inhabitant – the king of the island. So when the Italian king visited Sardinia the shepherd, as a present from one monarch to another, sent him several sheep. The real king was surprisingly delicate in his reply, not for a moment suggesting that the shepherd was lower in station than himself, but said that if he had need of the sheep he would have kept them. As it was, he graciously returned them and enquired if there was anything he could do for the shepherd in return. Our pastoral 'king' asked for a pound of gunpowder, which was immediately forthcoming. No one knows what the shepherd did with his royal gift, but looking at the island today one wonders how he and his sheep managed to survive on it at all.

North of Olbia it is 12 miles just to reach the end of the bay at Golfo Aranci, a fishing village and another car ferry terminus for Civitavecchia. But unless you are catching a boat you will take the alternative road north which leads directly to the Costa Smeralda, on a very pretty drive with the occasional small farmhouses set in the macchia scrub and the serrated rocky hills inland.

Suddenly, there is a sharp change in driving habits. In Olbia, despite the traffic snarl-up, a driver sees my Roman number plates and waits patiently while I reverse out of the flow and change direction. Here there is a dash and a dare and an expertise about the driving that is entirely lacking elsewhere on the island, and it is due largely to the fact that the drivers are Italian, not Sard. There are other differences, too. For a start, almost everyone can speak English. The entry to the Costa Smeralda is a lump of rock by the side of the road with the name engraved upon it, and similar natural sign-posting is used throughout. The architectural theme is to make villas, shops and hotels look as if they have grown out of their surroundings, and though purists may complain this is artificial and phony, the overall effect is discreet, luxurious, and an exclusive international playground which, with the strict controls now in operation, will stay that way.

The whole project, comprising several hundred acres and 35 miles of coastline – but by road it is ten minutes from one end to the other – is fairly recent. The Aga Khan and a group of friends decided to buy land in the early 1960s in the almost depopulated area and built their own homes, then formed a Consortium which gives them absolute control over who buys land and what they build where. It is by no means the feudal system it sounds. While the founder members of the Consortium have special voting rights, six votes for every 1000 square metres of land they hold, their regulations are entirely protective with a sensibility that any small land-owner would value.

In practical terms, this means that all telephone and electricity cables are carried underground, that no sewage is allowed to flow into the sea, and that the owner with 2400 square metres can use only 200 of those for his house. In other words, a ratio of about ten per cent building to 90 per cent land. Furthermore, the rocks, plants, shrubs and so on are carefully removed from the site before building starts and re-planted at its conclusion, which is one reason why gardens look so well established and in keeping with the surroundings.

Executives of the Costa Smeralda claim that it is not only the international jet set who benefit, but the Sards, too, many of whom are returning to Gallura having emigrated from what was once the poorest region in the island. In those days water was a problem. Since the development it comes quickly and directly from Lake Liscia about 20 miles distant. There is also, of course, permanent employment for the Sards themselves.

One of the first allied industries to be established was a ceramics factory at Olbia which employs 140 people and makes hand-painted ware for the hotels and villas using clay from Siniscola. A more difficult task is training staff. An hotel school has been opened at Arzachena and now has a couple of hundred students. Meanwhile the bulk of hotel staff are Italian. But slowly, Sards are beginning to take over the jobs. I met one farmer's daughter who before her arrival a couple of years ago could barely make a telephone call; now she is personal assistant to the public relations officer.

A whole range of other job opportunities have sprung up, from laundries and supermarkets to real estate, hire and sale of boats, management of port and harbour facilities, and so on. Employees living here have homes provided for them and schools for their children. In short, it is a new, self-contained community that need have little to do with the rest of the island. There are now ten hotels, not all de-luxe category, and about 240 villas, and it is expected that the continuing strict building policy will give the Costa Smeralda the lowest density of population in Sardinia come the year 2000.

Such exclusivity is expensive. Investment so far is at least £30m and there is more to come, notably 8m lire on construction of a second harbour, Port West. Dredging was proceeding apace during my visit and the completed port is to have berths for 470 boats up to 200 tons the year round, and there will be clubs, and facilities for refuelling as well as shipwrights. With the existing facilities at Porto Cervo, this should make the area one of the finest equipped yachting centres in the Mediterranean. It is already noted for superb sailing and the hope is that the international regatta calendar will expand along with the facilities.

Porto Cervo is the hub and indeed the only village on the Costa Smeralda. Its harbour and jetty encircle a pedestrians-only Piazza lined with shops and flats at two levels and backed by the Hotel Porto Cervo. The colours are faded blues, oranges, reds and yellows, and there is an inner octagonal courtyard with the Red Lion pub serving British brews. Without people it looks somewhat like a film set awaiting the stars, but it is on a scale that indicates it caters for large numbers.

From the piazza there is a little wooden bridge separating the inner canal moorings, mainly day boats, from the main yacht anchorage, and a path leads to the Cervo Tennis Club, which is building five more tennis courts to add to its existing two. The building is unostentatious and its facilities, on payment of daily, weekly or monthly fee, include indoor and outdoor pools, upstairs lounge for hire and snack restaurant, all handy amenities for villa-owners. Up the hill from Porto Cervo stretches Sa Conca arcade designed by Michele Busiri Vici of Rome, who was also the architect of an hotel and the church. Some of the shops have yet to be let and above and behind them are flats that look like houses cleverly built higgledy-piggledy fashion, so that each is slightly different from the next, though the façades are identical. The occupiers have a communal swimming pool completely hidden from view.

Stella Maris church, built in 1968, is a modern gem, though it is unjustly and mysteriously described in the literature as Vici's 'personal free plastic south Mediterranean style,' clearly a case of mis-translation. It is very small, only about 60-feet long and 40 feet wide, and inside has graceful rounded arches, a green granite floor and fascinating lights like delicate steel cones. Try and get the priest to switch on those lights, not merely to admire the effect but to look at El Greco's 'Mater Dolorosa' given in 1969 by Baroness Bentinck when her husband was Dutch Ambassador in Paris. She said then: 'I hope this gift will bring good fortune to the church and to the village of Porto Cervo.'

The Baroness's hopes for prosperity have certainly been realised, and not just for Porto Cervo. It is five miles south from here to an exotic hotel, designed by a Frenchman, Jacques Couelle in 1963 and named after the Cala di Volpe, the Bay of Foxes, which it overlooks with a delicate quartet of islands off-shore. The building is a surrealistic castle-style structure with rough walls of soft pink drifting into yellow, and the American car dealers, despite the slump in their industry at the time, are cheerfully amusing themselves prior to the opening of their convention.

As there were two jet-plane loads of them, it says something for the scale of Cala di Volpe that I wandered around its nooks and crannies and met no one. The crowds were gathered only in the gigantic main foyer, broken up by pillars, or out on the jetty setting off in motor boats. The hotel rambles on in a forgetful way, with windows and doors and staircases in odd corners, and a canal separates the smart boutiques from a row of rooms intended to look like stables.

Those Americans not boating are at the nearby Pevero Golf Club, with its English pro and a sharp contrast between the smooth green of the course and the rough macchia and rocky hills. The pro reckons it is among the top five courses in Europe, and just driving around in an American-made golf cart is a joy. The diminuitive clubhouse is due to be replaced, and there is a projected villa development behind the course.

At Cala di Petra Ruia, the Costa Smeralda ends, so retrace the short drive back through Labbiadori, a tiny hamlet inland which was not purchased by the Consortium, and a few miles north of Porto Cervo round the next bay, comically called Liscia di Vacca, though there are no cows to be seen, is the Pitrizza which is almost invisible from the landward approach and entirely so from the sea. The designer here was Luigi Vietti, and it is a collection of half a dozen cottages, (visited once by Princess Margaret); they are comfortable but not pretentious, the embroidery on sofas, armchairs and linen revealing the careful local workmanship. Each has its own garden and the whole atmosphere is designed to give the impression that the guests are staying in a private house, a theme carried through in the low-built public rooms which lead out on to a terrace and down to three sandy beaches. There is a swimming pool, and it is 50 feet above the level of the sea water with which it is filled. Its total discretion of design and appearance (most guests have titles), derives from three things: the one-storey-only scattered buildings; the use of local granite in soft browns, pinks and russets; and the entrancing addition of gardens on every flat roof, each one a miniature rockery with grass and plants and flowers cascading over the edge providing a perfect camouflage.

Beyond Pitrizza is the Punta Battistone which marks

the northern end of the Costa Smeralda and the beginning of the long fjord that ends at Arzachena, with its strange, turtle-shaped rock.

The 45-minute drive from here to Palau is through green scenery with distant mountains. Impatient motorists are held up twice by a 'commuter' train with two carriages that chugs gently along and seems to make the prospect of catching the 6.30 p.m. boat to La Maddalena an unlikely one. But the quayside is reached, the tickets bought, and a collection of last-minute cars and passengers hustled aboard for the 20-minute crossing.

La Maddalena with its archipelago was a vital defensive position in this part of the Mediterranean and today it has the largest naval training establishment in Italy, plus a NATO base that can repair nuclear submarines. Its history has connections with two of the world's most famous warriors: Napoleon Bonaparte, and Horatio Nelson who thought it was 'the *summum bonum* of everything which is valuable for us.' Napoleon's views could not have been so enthusiastic. He left Bonifacio in Corsica on 22 February 1793, as second-in-command of a French blockading force and landed during the night on the island of Santo Stefano, one of the archipelago, preparing to open fire on La Maddalena on the 24th.

But the town garrison of 500 replied too briskly, and the dismasted French frigate at the head of the force promptly made off for Arzachena, leaving Santo Stefano defenceless to the storming of 400 Sards from Palau. Their attack was so successful that Bonaparte was obliged to flee, leaving behind 200 prisoners and all his stores, baggage and artillery. The ignominious retreat was harassed by the enemy all the way and the occasion was the first major defeat of the young Corsican lieutenant.

The Straits of Bonifacio, separating the French island from Sardinia, the Romans called Fossa Fretum, meaning deep trench, but no one thought of apportioning the off-shore islands to the respective countries until 1760, when joint arbitrators decided the matter by simply taking an east-west line at mid-point between Capo lo Sprono in Corsica and Capo Falcone in Sardinia. All north of the line went French, all south – the larger number – Italian, which was a lucky thing for Nelson who happened past some 40 years later and otherwise would have been in a somewhat delicate position cruising about and not knowing which island of the archipelago belonged to whom.

In all, he spent 15 months around Agincourt Sound, as he called the Straits, hoping that the French fleet would emerge from Toulon and chasing every rumour that it had. Meanwhile he sat aboard *H.M.S. Victory* conducting a voluminous correspondence with naval and government personnel in England on the merits of Sardinia as the place from which England could control the Mediterranean; and an equally voluminous one with the various victualling masters on the subject of the fleet's requirements, this latter chore revealing not only a unique view of what La Maddalena was like in those days, but a meticulous attention to the smallest detail that concerned the welfare of his navy.

Nelson lost no opportunity to hammer home his reasons why La Maddalena was a better base than Malta, and indeed he had been there exactly a week when he was writing to Sir Alexander John Ball at Malta: 'This anchorage is certainly one of the best I have met with for a fleet – water, brooms, sand, onions, some beef, plenty of sheep ... ' A month later he was pressing the point to Lord Hobart in London: 'This, which is the finest island in the Mediterranean, possesses harbours fit for arsenals, and of a capacity to hold our navy within 24 hours sail of Toulon ... no fleet could pass to the eastward between Sicily and the coast of Barbary, nor through the Faro of Messina.'

While he himself never set foot ashore, despite a doubtful legend that he had an affair with a local girl, Emma Lion, he nevertheless felt able to assure the English government of the great potential:

God knows if we could possess one island, Sardinia, we should want neither Malta nor any other. The country is fruitful beyond idea, and abounds in cattle, sheep and would in corn, wine and oil. In the hands of a liberal government and freed from the dread of the Barbary states, there is no telling what its produce would not amount to. It is worth any money to obtain, and I pledge my existence it could be held for as little as Malta in its establishment and produce a larger revenue.

The prevailing situation at La Maddalena proved a little less fruitful than this eulogistic description. Before Carlo Emanuele III took possession of it and the adjacent islands in 1767 only a few shepherds had managed to eke out a precarious living. Nelson refers to their being a 'village of 40 or 50 small houses', but the sheep, on closer inspection, turned out to be below the standard required by the English navy being 'very small, meagre and inferior in quality.' A luckless captain who bought five live bullocks, 300lb of onions and six bags of hay was severely reprimanded by Nelson, first for the unauthorized purchase and secondly for the unwarranted extravagance of buying food for animals that were to be slaughtered immediately.

Meanwhile, the navy's victuallers at Gibraltar and Malta were kept busy with a shopping list containing the most precise minutiae not only of the items required but of the quality of those items, the latter often being checked out on arrival at La Maddalena. Following the arrival of one consignment from Malta, Nelson instructed the masters of his ships: 'You are hereby directed to take a most strict and careful survey on the pork ... and in order to judge of the meat when boiled, that it does not shrink more than the pork used in the navy, you are hereby required to take a certain number of pieces, out of one or more of the casks, promiscuously, as they come to hand, and boil them on board the Senior Officer's ship. You will also take a bushel of pease, in the same way, from one or more of the bags, and see them also boiled, paying very particular attention that neither the pork nor pease are too much done.'

On the question of health, Nelson, whose own was in bad shape, did everything possible to avoid his men being sick. Those sailors in the naval hospital at Malta were provided with milk in their tea, morning and evening, on his instructions, and those with him at La Maddalena were lucky enough to be in a place where there was no malaria. The perennial problem of scurvy was not so easily dealt with, but the Commander-in-Chief consulted the doctor, then prescribed that each man who had scurvy should be given 6oz of lemon juice and 2oz of sugar daily for 12 days. At the end of this time, Nelson required to know whether the treatment had been successful.

While this was going on, there were the constant comings and goings of the fleet in their long pursuit of the French that was to end with the Battle of Trafalgar, and at various times orders went to ships to stand by in case of imminent attack. One rumour had it that the French would attack La Maddalena itself, so Nelson sent a bomb-vessel to hove-to with instructions to the captain to post guard rowing boats during the night and to help and protect the governor should this become necessary. There was also the delicate question of Britain's role in effecting the possible escape of the King and Queen of Naples, and detailed notes went from Nelson to another captain on how he should act.

Globally, Nelson realised the advantage to England if Russia went to war with France. The King of Sardinia's neutrality would then, as the admiral saw it, be at an end, and it might be possible to persuade him to have English troops landed at La Maddalena and thus hold the northern part of Sardinia against a Corsican invasion. Further, Nelson went into the King's financial position, pointing out that royalty was receiving very poor revenue from Sardinia, of the order of £5,000 a year, whereas if the King ceded the island to England he would get £500,000, giving him an income of £25,000 a year. A circuitous way of trying to get a naval base at La Maddalena!

The fleet finally left the archipelago on 19 January, 1805, and after cruising around Sardinian waters until the end of March, followed the French to the West Indies. A few months before, however, the Commander-in-Chief of the English navy in the Mediterranean made a present to the church of La Maddalena and, when thanked for it, promised the inhabitants: 'These little ornaments are nothing. Wait till I catch the French outside their port. If they will but come out I am sure to capture them and I promise to give you the value of one of their frigates to build a church.'

Nelson's death at the Battle of Trafalgar prevented him from keeping his promise, and the church has since been rebuilt with other monies. But the 'little ornaments' are still in it, though to find them requires some determination. I begin my enquiries confidently enough outside the town hall in Piazza Garibaldi, having in fact already seen the church round the corner in Piazza S. Maria Maddalena but discarded it as being too modern. A cheerful lady shopper, emerging from the market adjacent to the Palazzo Comunale, took me firmly by the hand and frog-marched me whence I had come.

'There,' she said, pointing at Santa Maddalena, a 1934 building with an imposing façade. 'Nelson?' I queried, she nodded vigorously. Inside, the altar was decorated with pink gladioli and it is clear that the back of the church and the bell-tower are original. An investigation of every nook and cranny failed to reveal a crucifix and a pair of silver candlesticks with the Bronte Arms upon them. Back to the main square, and this time my informant was, appropriately, a naval lieutenant who spoke excellent French. He knew his historical onions and, what is more, was certain the priest would be there at 5.30 p.m. to open the sacristy wherein the treasures lie, as mass was to be celebrated half an hour later.

Back at the appointed hour, there was no sign of the priest, but a little old lady in black grasped what the visitor wanted and took me into a dim, dusty back room where, in a plain bookcase, are Nelson's gifts, battered, worn and unpolished, plus a letter from him, dated *Victory*, 18 October 1804, which, unlike the gifts, is so well preserved that I was able to take it down in its entirety:

I have to request that I may be allowed to present to the church at Maddalena a piece of church plate as a small token of my esteem for the worthy inhabitants and of my remembrance of the hospitable treatment His Majesty's fleet under my command has ever received from them; May God Bless us all. I remain, dear sir, your most obedient servant, Nelson and Bronte.

Two postscripts indicate that the gift will be presented by the Rev. Dr. Scott, Nelson's chaplain.

Some of that 'hospitable treatment' could have come the navy's way in La Maddalena's main shopping street, Via Azuni, which is just behind the quayside so through the alleyways is a view of sparkling water and white ferry boats. The fishing harbour is round the corner from the ferry terminus at Cala Gavetta with private yachts moored here, too, and lots of traffic rushing through the Piazza P. Tommaso which fronts on to it and has a garage in the middle into which petrol is being ponderously delivered in drums.

Most of the hotels are beyond this point, a short walk from the town centre, and the one I was staying in, which must take the prize for the most unkempt, uncaring, sluttish and sleazy establishment anywhere in Sardinia, had a resigned clientele of American NATO staff living there while they looked for a home. At a quayside restaurant, eating a mixed sea food platter, I met one of the Americans who had been here for six months, preceded by two years in Greece. There is an American school, but he was sending his nine-year-old son to the Italian one instead.

The panoramic route around the island poses the problem of which deserted beach, out of the fresh winds, to choose. Perhaps in the height of summer they may be crowded, but in mid-May there is not a soul at Spalmatore with its little jetty, and a brave friend swam while I paddled. There are tiny hamlets all over the island, clusters of half-a-dozen pink or white one-storey houses sticking up from the macchia that covers the ground so well it looks like overgrown moss.

The northern end of La Maddalena presents quite a surprise, for after a series of remote coves is Porto Massimo with its bay, jetty a few yachts and a brand new development. The beige terraced houses stand around a piazza and at one side is a hotel built in the same style so that it looks like a big brother to the houses. It is a fine modern building, at the moment completely empty. The whole route, including beach stop, need take no more than a couple of hours.

To reach Caprera island, take the road east through the barracks in the suburbs, which gives you some idea of the size of the naval establishment. Under the Fascists visitors were not encouraged because the base was intended to serve as a springboard for the occupation of Corsica. Ironically, Mussolini was held here for a few days in 1943. The Passo della Moneta is the causeway that links the two islands, with the wind whipping up the waves around the rocks that stick up everywhere in the water.

The tamarisk-lined drive the other side of the causeway leads directly to the house of Giuseppe Garibaldi, Italy's great nineteenth-century hero who became owner of Caprera and for nearly 30 years regarded it as his home and refuge until his death on 2 June 1882. Historians say that without him the cause of Italian unity would have been lost, and as a tactician in guerilla warfare, perfected in the South American pampas, he was the ideal revolutionary of the day. He reached his island by a most circuitous route, around the world in fact, engaged largely upon sea-faring activities but taking up other jobs, including chandling, when shipping employment was low, and always awaiting the call to arms.

Garibaldi's parents had planned that he should enter the church, but after a brief trip from his home town of Nice by ship to Genoa he pleaded with his father to let him become a sailor. In his mid-twenties he joined the recently formed Italian youth organisation which in 1843 attempted an unsuccessful uprising. Garibaldi was condemned to death, escaped to America and began 20 years of exile, during which time he helped the South Americans in their fight for independence in Uruguay and the Rio Grande, and met and married Anita in 1842 in Montevideo.

He was back in Europe, though, for a major campaign

in 1849, leading the patriots from the northern Italian provinces to the defence of Rome and when that failed taking to the mountains of the Apennines with a band of followers. He eluded his enemies – Naples, Spain, France and Austria – but, tragically, his wife died in his arms and he fled to Piedmont, not with any idea of seeking permanent asylum, but as a temporary refuge not too far from his motherless children at Nice. The Piedmontese Government packed him off to Tunis, where the Bey refused him, so he was put ashore at La Maddalena, where he spent a happy month, though at that stage any idea of settling on Caprera seems to have been far from his mind.

His next port of call was Tangier, where he spent six months as a guest of the Piedmontese consul, and used the time to write his South American memoirs. By June 1850 he was on his way again to the Americas, this time to the North, to get a temporary job as a journeyman chandler in a factory on Staten Island before heading off round the world via China and Australasia, where he was most impressed with Tasmania. Then came a real seaman's job, that of captain of the 1200-ton *Common-wealth,* bound for Newcastle. Garibaldi's reputation as a champion of European democracy was already establish-ed, particularly on Tyneside where the workers apparently listened entranced to lectures in Italian and applauded loudly whenever they understood the odd word, usually Garibaldi's name.

When the miners heard their hero would be arriving to collect a cargo of coal they brought him a sword of honour and sent a deputation on board the *Commonwealth* to deliver the gift. Garibaldi replied in English: 'One of the people, a workman like yourselves, I value very highly these expressions of your esteem, the most so because you testify thereby your sympathy with my poor, oppressed and down-trodden country. Italy will one day be a nation, and its free citizens will know how to acknow-ledge all the kindness shown her exiled sons in the days of her darkest troubles.'

The time was not yet ripe, though, and Garibaldi pass-ed the next year at Nice, combining a paternal line in family duties by teaching his younger son, Ricciotti, to read, while passing the evenings in the company of an English widow. The death of his brother, Felici, in 1855, gave him the capital to fulfill his dream of building a house in solitude, and his first choice on Sardinia was Capo Testa, near Santa Teresa di Gallura. Friends at La Maddalena pointed out that this would be far too dangerous, claiming that he could easily be carried off from there by Corsicans, and, surprisingly, Garibaldi heeded their advice and bought the northern half of Caprera for about £360.

It was a perfect place from every point of view. Personally, he had the wildness of scenery and the tranquillity he craved, but it was only an hour's rowing time to La Maddalena where the Piedmontese navy often called and could collect him if he was wanted for a campaign. So he had all the advantages of a hermit's life, while being in touch with his friends and available should the need arise. In 1856 he and his eldest son, Menotti, moved to Caprera and lived in a tent while they put up the little wooden house, still there, as a temporary home for his favourite daughter, Teresita.

Another year passed before the real house, in South American architectural style, could be lived in, and its upper storey lasted but a few years against the island's strong winds before being dismantled. Garibaldi was not the only inhabitant of the island. The descendants of a bandit called Ferraciolo also lived on Caprera and were on excellent terms with the new-comer; not so the other occupant, an Englishman named Collins. The trouble arose because the livestock of each trespassed equally upon the other's land.

The exile was a keen market-gardener and it was not long before the goats and pigs of Collins found their way to the Italian's potato and cabbage patch. Equally, the goats which Garibaldi had imported from Malta roamed freely across the other's territory. Finally, Garibaldi built a wall from west to east across Caprera, said to be his most successful effort at masonry! Luckily, Collins died in 1859 and his widow, reputedly a much less cantankerous character, moved to La Maddalena. Five years later English admirers bought the exile the other half of the island from Mrs. Collins.

Although ships crossed from Genoa to La Maddalena only once a month, the house was often overflowing with guests, who were required to lend a hand in the garden and, on occasion, search for lost lambs. The host himself drank nothing but water or milk, but his visitors had access to a wine cellar and, by all accounts, a laden table. The idyllic existence was broken off in 1860, when he set sail for his successful expedition to Sicily that solved the question of Italian unity, and he appeared then for the first time wearing his distinctive "uniform" of grey loose trousers, a red shirt tucked in at the waist, a silk handkerchief around his neck and a voluminous grey poncho.

On Caprera the garden is still laid out approximately as it was in his day with, in the centre of the courtyard, an enormous tree he planted to celebrate the birth of his daughter Clelia in 1867. The last of his children to survive, she died aged 92 on February 2, 1959, and is buried in the family cemetery a short distance from the house. The tombs require a little explanation, for although Garibaldi was devoted to his first wife, Anita, and she gave him four children – Menotti, Teresita, Rosita and Ricciotti – after her death he had something of a roving eye.

There was the English widow at Nice to whom he was engaged for a time. There was Battistina Ravella whom he did not marry, but who gave him a daughter whom he called Anita. Then there was a disastrous marriage to the Contessa Raimundi, a young woman who had brought him news of the Austrians when he was hiding in the Apennines. The ceremony, in 1860, did not even get past the wedding night, for the 52-year-old bridegroom discovered a letter the Contessa had written to another man and told her: 'Then see that you do not bear my name. I leave you for ever.' They separated immediately, but the marriage was not annulled until 20 years later in 1880, and a couple of weeks later Garibaldi married his last love, Francesca Armosina, who had already borne him three children – Clelia, Rosita and

Manlio.

So the tombs to be seen at Caprera include those of Teresita, the first and favourite daughter, his illegitimate daughter Anita who died when she was 16, two year old Rosita and his third wife, Francesca by his specific request. They are all in plain marble, with the exception of Garibaldi's which, like the man himself, is a rough-hewn lump of granite crudely shaped with a pair of fresh lilies placed daily upon it and traditionally guarded by a sailor.

In mid-May there is a lot of construction going on around the Casa Garibaldi. The path to the cemetery has been done up with a low stone wall flanked by palm trees and beyond this the diseased olive trees that form a buffer between the cultivated garden and the rocky macchia hinterland are being cut down and the grass turned to furrows. The gardeners are working fast with machetes, breaking into song every so often, and laying aside the green grass to take home for fodder. They draw my attention to an open-sided shed containing the boat given to Garibaldi by Emanuele II and a smaller white one that beloned to one of his sons.

Around Clelia's pine tree in the courtyard are tamarisks and an herbaceous border. Sadly, the house itself is closed for major repairs but I peep in through the carved wooden front door to see fine wooden ceilings and red tiled floors. The custodian has little time to explain anything because he is engaged upon a violent and splen-did altercation with a group of workmen digging a nar-row trench outside the garden wall. The argument had been volatile on my arrival, and I had waited some moments for a lull to catch the custodian's eye to unlock the gate. Emerging an hour later it is still raging, the workers have thrown down their tools and are leaning sullenly up against the wall surveying their plumb line which might, or there again might not, have been the cause of the dispute.

Round the corner from the quarrel is the view Garibaldi had from his house and I have been gazing across at La Maddalena and down to the shoreline of Caprera for some minutes before I realise that at the water's edge is the discreet Club Mediterranée – there is another one on Santo Stefano. Its round thatched-roof rondavels have bamboo walls and a door, but no windows, and more are being built among the eucalyptus trees. It is a remote and peaceful setting, the rock roses growing anything up to waist-high in places.

Gravel roads run north to south on Caprera and the naval presence becomes more obvious going south towards Punta Rossa; clearly these cars and lorries are not out for a pleasure drive. Along the coast there is tamarisk afforestation and shortly afterwards a barred gate leading to the naval station. The road north stops equally sharply, though there is no naval presence, and without a picnic to linger beneath the sweet-smelling pines, there is no reason to delay further, but return to La Maddalena and pick up one of the frequent ferries back to the mainland and Palau.

The scenery north from here is benign and pastoral all the way to Santa Teresa di Gallura which in the fourteenth century was called Longone, after the castle the Aragonese built but lost in 1388 to Eleonora d'Arborea. A mere three years later the castle was back in Aragonese hands and they held on to it until 1410 when Cassiano Doria, then overlord of Castel Genovese (Castel Sardo), thought to expand and succeeded in expelling the Aragon colony.

They recovered it in 1420, for a couple of years, but the Genoese then captured and raided the castle. When the King of Aragon finally got possession he decided to diminish its strength – and therefore its worth to the enemy – by demolishing both castle and fortifications, which he did in 1433. There was a long tranquil period of 400 years until the Piedmontese repopulated the place with their own colony in 1810 and, to commemorate this final occupation, changed its name to Villa Teresa, after Maria Teresa, the wife of Vittorio Emanuele, King of Sardinia.

One fortification only is left in Santa Teresa today, and that is the sixteenth-century Torre Longosardo built by the Spanish King Philip II, which overlooks the fine beach of Rena Bianca, the resort area where holidaymakers have one of the finest sunset views of Corsica to the north-east. After the disappointment of La Maddalena's hotel, Santa Teresa's stop-over is magnificent. The meal begins with cold courgettes and artichokes stuffed with bread, herbs and cheese; continues with spaghetti with a clam, parsley and tomato sauce; is followed by half a dozen fresh clams and the main dish of sea bream mayonnaise, all washed down with a fine white wine.

The little town sits on top of the hill and does not overlook the beach.In the Piazza San Vittorio is the nineteenth-century church, and the hub is the Piazza Vittorio Emanuele I, its centre paved and tree-lined. It is a sleepy scene and it seems to bear no relation to the third section of Santa Teresa, the port, retaining the old name of Porto Longone, which is a mile away and is a long creek where boats tie up from Corsica (one hour to Bonifacio) and La Maddalena (also one hour). The most interesting aspect of the port is that the development is on one side only – the quayside with its tamarisk trees, lobsters awaiting export and bustle of arriving ferries. Across the water, only a few yards away, is simply hilly countryside, giving the impression that the smaller boats have found the sheltered natural anchorage by accident and moored where they please.

From Santa Teresa a road runs the three miles to Capo Testa – Garibaldi's first home choice – via rugged scenery and the quiet bay of S. Reparata which the Pisans used as a harbour and is now a development of villas, shops and restaurants. The Cape, with its lighthouse, is even more rugged and windy. Back in Santa Teresa, the coast road runs south-west crossing endless rivulets and passing beach after beach with access paths and tightly-packed tamarisks for windbreaks, to reach Castel Sardo in a little over 40 miles and thence Sassari.

9 Nuoro

Nuoro, more than the other Sardinian cities, is part of its province, without the sharp divisions between urbanites and country folk. Nobody could claim that of itself it is a top tourist attraction, though it does have a spectacular mountain setting. The interest lies not in historical sights, but in its people who have given it two major claims to fame. The city has produced the island's greatest literary figures, and its outlying villages have produced the most celebrated bandits.

Its artistic life continues to flourish and has a real originality uninfluenced by invaders or conquerors. Almost everyone seems to lead a 'double-life', singing, writing, painting when there is any sort of pause in the work by which they earn a living. The few who put neither pen to paper nor brush to canvas are ardent conversationalists, again reflecting their isolated region and independent lives, and the topics that dominate any talk are politics and banditry. They are completely honest about the latter, making no attempt to hide its existence, and indeed discuss the latest crime figures or well-known vendettas with a disarming frankness.

But then the Sards have always regarded the subject more in the category of quixotic outlawry than grand larceny. Until recently banditry was a personal matter of Sard against Sard in the form of vengeance and vendetta, usually sparked-off by cattle- or sheep-rustling. Now it is changing to people-stealing, rich industrialists and land-owners proving more lucrative in the way of ransom than animals. Cattle-theft goes back to Roman times; indeed one of the reasons given for the expulsion of the Jews from Italy to Sardinia was that they would, somehow, help to put down the bandits.

No alien, however, stands a chance against the native mountain people, skilled as they are in living off the land – even if it is somebody else's land! – and with an unparalleled knowledge of their hostile terrain. It was, and is, classic guerilla warfare, with a large number of carabinieri from the mainland having only limited success in combating the crime figures. The police bustle about in their jeeps, and perhaps should be called the Highwayman Patrol, but no Sard will inform to a 'foreigner', i.e. an Italian, even about a sworn enemy.

The dogs which the Romans brought in to try and track down the Barbaracini, a corruption of the Roman term Barbaria, are still in the mountains, now converted to sheep-dogs but looking no more friendly than centuries ago. Then, as now, livestock was all-important, but as there was very little fencing and few land-boundaries the pigs, sheep and cows roamed freely making themselves easy targets for thieves. The deprived animal-owner hunted down and killed the robber, then himself fled. The dead man's family demanded revenge and as soon as a son was old enough he would continue the vendetta. It led, of course, to situations where the slate could never be wiped clean, each side perpetuating the feud so that there was always a killing to be avenged.

Some twentieth-century outlaws are spoken of with pride, and when a famous bandit who, like Robin Hood, was said to have robbed the rich to give to the poor, was finally arrested in the 1960s he was first flown to Cagliari to appear on television that evening! There is even supposed to be in existence an unwritten code of laws dealing with brigandage, vendettas and livestock which, among other things, stipulates death for an informer. Nothing has changed dramatically here since the Middle Ages, when the entire island population was around half a million with an annual slaughter rate of one in 500. Nuoro Province, which has the lowest population density, is credited with maintaining Sardinia's position as the place with the highest murder rate in Italy.

Two mountain villages, Orgosolo and Orune, share the

dubious title of 'bandit capitals' of the island; it was from the former that the celebrated outlaw came who appeared on television; and the latter has communal land on which to graze stolen livestock before taking it to the butcher at nearby Nuoro. Cattle-rustling has been partially solved by a ruling that all animals must be branded with the mark of their commune and that the owner has to produce a certificate for each one. But meat on the hoof can be transformed into meat on the butcher's slab before anyone catches up with it.

The shepherds try to protect their stock by insuring it and thus recovering something like three-quarters of the value of the stolen animal from the insurance company. They also band together to patrol their pastures, all of which has helped to lower and diminish cattle-rustling as a profession. Unlike the wine co-operatives, however, the mountain farmers as yet show little sign of getting together for economic survival. They own almost half the pasture land but much of it is in scattered parcels and in any case they have the stubborn Sard pride which makes them believe they would lose face if they merged with the others.

All these pastoral problems are highly relevant to the provincial capital, Nuoro, for it is a city where cows graze in downtown meadows, where occasional horsemen gallop through the streets and where modern office blocks conceal vital meetings about cheese and wine, the two products for which the province is famed. Nuoro the city is famed for its costume museum, one of the few sights, and the tourist board makes no apology for the fact that it is closed and no date has been set for its re-opening. They assure me, and prove to be right, that I will be able to see the costumes being worn, which will be much better than the museum.

Traditions live long with the Nuorese. Not for them an easy acquiescence to foreign domination and the first invaders to try, the Romans, succeeded only in disposing of a mixed bag of Carthaginians and Sards in 215 B.C., killing 12,000 and taking 3,600 prisoners. To conquer the territory was another matter. The Barbaracini, as they came to be known, went on rebelling – and losing large numbers of their population as a result – until the end of the third century A.D., by which time the Roman Emperor Diocletian was murdering converts to Christianity and laying a base for the inordinate number of saints Sardinia claims today.

The mountain folk, in fact, took to the new religion rather late, and it seems that relinquishing their pagan rites was one of the peace terms the then governor of the island demanded of them through their chief. But certainly towards the end of the sixth century A.D. Gregory the Great was sending congratulatory letters to the Sard converts. The history of the Nuorese then remains a closed book until the Aragonese domination of Sardinia, when they refused either to recognise or pay tribute to Alfonso V, Aragon King.

Somehow, no one took action to get the tributes until 1719, when the Spaniards demanded a double contribution from the people of Nuoro Province. The response from the Nuorese was to move wives, children and valuables up into the mountains and keep the overlords entirely at bay. Only with the establishment of the House of Savoy did the Barbaracini return to their villages. The fact that they have never been really subjugated is reflected in the dialect they speak today, some of which is pure Latin; indeed a Latin dictionary could prove a good deal more useful than an Italian one, except that if you look lost in Nuoro the population will be at your side in a moment.

Their pride in the city extends to an intimate knowledge of their two famous literary figures, whose biographies they will relate while leading you by the hand to the homes each occupied. Sebastiano Satta, the poet, who died in 1914, had a big house – still lived in – alongside the Piazza named after him. The square itself has been turned into a sort of modern open-air sculpture gallery with strange pieces of granite dotted about, each piece with a tiny bronze figure inset into a carved niche if a natural ledge does not present itself.

Alas for the home of Grazia Deledda, Nobel prize-winning novelist of 1926, it is shuttered and dilapidated. I am told her novels of Nuorese life are as apt now as when they were written in the early 1920s, and although she married a Roman and lived in that city for a time, she returned to her home town to write in a little garden house, the tiled roof of which, covered in wistaria and roses, can be seen over the wall from the Via Grazia Deledda.

Next door is the family home, a rather elegant house on three floors but in a derelict condition. The tourist board tells me the city has bought both properties and intends to restore them. The church the novelist often mentioned in her books is the one in which she is buried. Our Lady of Solitude was originally built in 1625, but has since been altered beyond recognition. It is now a simple pretty little white church on the outskirts of Nuoro en route for Monte Ortobene. Deledda's name is commemorated by an annual literary prize.

Nuoro became the capital city of the province in 1926, which is perhaps why the cathedral, of an earlier date, nicely situated on a hilly square with grass and small oak trees, is a rather uninteresting building firmly locked. There is no central quarter here, but the main shopping street, Corso Garibaldi, doubles as the promenade area of an evening. One or two old buildings survive among the shops and smart boutiques. It is worth checking whether the Regional Costume Museum, so splendidly sign-posted, is open, though someone told me they had made four attempts and been told on each occasion that it was still being restored and the costumes were still being kept in Rome.

At nearly 2000 feet up this provincial capital is one of the highest cities in Italy, and the altitude makes for a cool, healthy climate. Even so, the Nuorese drive still higher to their playground on Monte Ortobene, a few miles through spectacular countryside and with the best hotels. As my trip had been arranged 'spontaneously', a favourite word of the Nuorese, and I had been virtually abducted into the province earlier than expected in order to attend the bandits' festival, the tourist board had not had time to inspect personally the accommodation up the mountain.

To their dismay, it came down to a room with a view

but without a bath, or a room with a bath but without a view. They began to worry that they had taken spontaneity too far! In vain did I assure them that the problem was not a major one, but their concern is typical of their attitude to visitors. It even goes as far as putting the sugar in the coffee for you and up at Monte Ortobene the smiling gentle waitress took one helpful step fruther. The first delicious course at dinner was a soft wafer-bread pancake, open, and covered with a tomato and herb sauce topped by a fried egg. This is not, however, how it is to be eaten; the girl took my knife and fork, broke and spread the egg, then folded up the sides of the wafer to make a neat envelope. We both admired this, then she touchingly cut the first piece for me and handed me back my knife and fork.

The biggest day of the year for Nuoro takes place on the mountain, and it is the Feast of the Redemption on 29 August, which is celebrated at the base of a 24-foot-high bronze statue of Christ, within walking distance of the Monte Ortobene hotels. After the religious part of the festival comes the costume parade, a folklore celebration and an exhibition of wines and carpets. It is, I am assured, a most spontaneous occasion.

10   Province of Nuoro

Along with its curious shape, ensuring that it has a bit of coast on each side of the island, the Province of Nuoro presents other oddities in the most interesting way, but it demands that visitors look for themselves, often behind the frontage, as it were. The mountains are impressive enough by themselves – rising to just over 6000 feet and romantically called Gennargentu, a Latin derivation meaning Silver Gate from the snow's reflection – but hidden inside is a labyrinth of rivers and caves, the latter being the secret hideaways of the early Sards.

Its eastern coastline is splendidly craggy, daring invaders to get a foothold, yet take a boat on a calm day and behind the forbidding cliffs is the inner enchanted world of the grottoes, with caverns and strange rock formations in exquisite colours and the last place in the Mediterranean where live seals survive from the Ice Age. Even the western coast, which is a very brief snippet of land, has the only navigable river on the island.

When it comes to food, these mountain folk produce some highly original dishes, though the ingredients could deter those with delicate appetites, based as they are on intestines and sheep's stomach. The shepherds have adapted their menus to suit their nomadic lives, so while they make a fine cottage-style cheese for export, they themselves eat a hard variety that will last for weeks. Both visitor and native drink the aptly named 'black' wine – dark red and very strong – which pops up at any time of the day, with or without a snack.

Although the people of Nuoro Province have a more distinctly corporate identity as a group than other parts

of Sardinia, the exception is the narrow strip of land out on a limb which leads to their western coastline. Its history is quite different from that of the mountainous interior. Starting, then, at the furthest western extremity, is Bosa Marina, at the mouth of the River Temo, whose diminutive Rossa Island with its lighthouse is now joined to the mainland by a pier. Round the corner from the little harbour you can hardly see the sand for the tightly-packed beach huts used by the holiday occupiers of the large old-fashioned villas.

Two miles winding upstream is Bosa itself, both a Carthaginian and a Roman settlement before being refounded by the Malaspina family in 1112. They built the Castle of Serravalle, subject, like most of Sardinia's mediaeval fortifications, to a history of vicissitudes and wars, passing from the Genoese to the Giudice of Arborea in 1308, and back again, and then to the Aragons, being finally annexed by Philip of Spain in 1565. Not surprisingly, the inhabitants of the town are people of mixed blood. The walk from the Piazza del Carmine up to the castle is a delightful 20 minutes or so, past hay being cut on the steep slopes beneath olive trees, and finally along a flower-filled path.

If you are lucky, the custodian will have spotted your slow ascent and be waiting at the gates with a bunch of gigantic keys. He lives in a tiny house in the open courtyard with a flock of pigeons and his own vine and broad bean patch in which poppies and sunflowers have joined. Serravalle, consequently, looks menacing only from the town below. Up here, all that is left of the castle is half a tower and the battlements from which any invasion by sea or land could easily be sighted.

On the stroll down there is a bird's eye view of tiny roof gardens, most with a vine, a patch of onions and a few pots of flowers, in a space about six feet long and three feet wide. The cathedral from here looks as if the domes and bell-tower have barely room to breathe, and it is situated just off the cobbled, pedestrians-only Corso Vittorio Emanuele II, where some of the tall houses are as old as the castle and have double doors which open on to stone-flagged entrance halls. Geraniums and pot plants liven up the wrought-iron balconies and here the laundry is actually strung across the street.

Lots of narrow alleyways lead off the Corso, with first-floor rooms built across to act as a linking bridge-head. The town is famous for its leather-work and there is a saddler sitting quietly and picturesquely at work in the street. Down on the quayside lined with palms the fishermen are busy too, seated in pairs with the nets spread over their knees to mend.

The boats are moored along one side and across the water is a row of half-abandoned warehouses. The Temo is not only the longest river in Sardinia, it is the only navigable one. To leave Bosa, cross the broad river by the old stone bridge and turn almost immediately left up the lane that leads to the gem of San Pietro Extramuros, which was founded in 1073 by Bishop Constantino di Castra and enlarged and modified in the thirteenth century by the Cistercians, who then occupied a nearby monastery of which there is now no trace.

To one side is an appealing farmhouse with a sloping red roof and first-floor verandah with red pillars. There is a flourishing market garden of lettuce, artichokes and fruit, and the custodian market garden of lettuce, arti-chokes and fruit, and the custodian of the church, not surprisingly, turns out to be the farmer, who wipes the mud from his boots before opening the main door. The interior is simple and unadorned, and clearly San Pietro is no longer in everyday use. The central nave is the original eleventh-century part, with stone pillars in pinky pastel colours, each block of stone a slightly different shade. The ceiling is wooden, the floor plain stone and the slender side naves have rough brick rounded ceilings, a later addition.

Return up the lane and turn left onto the main road which runs through soft hills with fields of figs and arti-chokes, crossing the railway several times before reaching Sindia, where outside the village there is another San Pietro, twelfth-century, also built by the Cistercians. They had an abbey here too, Santa Maria di Corte, built in 1147, which was abandoned in the fifteenth century. Five miles further on, over a bare plateau with

unclassified nuraghe lying about, is Macomer, built on a
ridge and backed by the plateau of Altopiano Campeda.
It is here that the famous Venus statue dating from 1500
B.C. was found and it can be seen in Cagliari museum.

In Roman times the town was called Macopissa and
was a military centre as well as an important stopover on
the road from Cagliari to Porto Torres. Two Roman
milestones in front of the sixteenth-century Aragonese-
gothic church commemorate this early history. The battle
won here by the Spaniards in 1478 ended Sardinian
independence. Today Macomer is an agricultural area,
with cattle-breeding, dairy products and wool. But it has
a later historical tale to tell, that of the Englishman,
Benjamin Pearce (sometimes called Piercy), who built the
railways, a matter that was continually postponed and
delayed as the various companies involved dissolved and
changed. Certainly Pearce became chief engineer in 1870
and a decade later the railway was completed, eight years
before his death in London. His son, Robert Charles
Pearce, took his place.

This much is documented, but what is still a cause for
conjecture, and legend, is the origin of Pearce's Indian
girl-friend. There are, as in all things Sard, several versions of the story, all equally fascinating. In one Pearce is
said to have been an officer in the English Army who
served in India and eloped with the daughter of a
maharajah bringing her to Europe. In another version
Pearce is said to have had nothing to do with the army,
but to have been a railway builder in England and married to Sarah Davies who bore him nine children, the last
born in Sardinia in 1873.

That would seem to contradict the Indian princess
theory, but there was an Indian girl, possibly a servant,
who came to Sardinia and died before Pearce could
complete a house for her. That house is now the railway
hotel at Macomer and though its restaurant is working
the rest of the building has a shabby derelict look. No
one has heard of Benjamin Pearce, though an old lady
speaking nothing but Sard inexplicably produces an
English pension book.

The Indian woman outlived Pearce by many years and

is said to have been a good and charitable woman. But what was her name? One story insists that it was Chilivani, the name of the railway junction north-east of Macomer and named after her by engineer Pearce. The anti-Pearce lobby not only claim that the delays in building the railway were partly due to him, because he wanted to prevent the track from running through his land, but state firmly that Chilivani is not an Indian name at all, but a bastardisation of another place in Sardinia called Cellevane. Opt for whichever you fancy!

From Macomer it is a little less than ten miles to the turn-off to Bolotana, which is sited at the junction point of two mountain ranges, Goceano and Marghine. Bolotana was founded by refugees from the then-important ecclesiastical town of Ottana, who fled there during a civil war in 1317 and for a time had a temporary settlement at Bolotana before building permanent homes. To reach Nuoro is just over 20 miles, and this provincial capital is the best base from which to tour most of the rest of the province.

On the map, the roads in the region have an ominously wiggly look, but distances are not daunting and with a little planning it is rarely necessary to return over the same route. An exception might be Oliena, which is only 20 minutes through olive groves and prickly pear hedges from Nuoro, because the inhabitants so delay the visitor with their hospitality and their wine – a lethal combination – that to return the same way is safer! The wine co-operative, one of 50 on the island, insists on a thorough tasting before 10 a.m., but wisely produces its lighter rosés before introducing the Nero black wine, very dry and heavy and never sold until it has been in the bottle for five years. The first gift of the day is two black bottles.

In the villages the vines are growing up the walls of the houses like wistaria and later in the day I wait in the main square, Piazza Jean Palache, with its fountain, to meet the local tourist association. All males over 30 wear a 'uniform' of brown corduroy trousers and jacket and cap, and most are seated in the Piazza on the stone benches, ignoring the political slogans scrawled on nearby walls calling for a free Sardinia, by which they mean home rule and the end of any control by the Italian Government.

The reception committee is five strong, and before anything else we repair to the home of one of them for another welcome-to-Oliena glass of Nero. This is served in tiny tumblers, a wise precaution in view of its strength, and is followed by an extraordinary version of the same wine which, after a period of about eight years, turns white, increases in alcoholic degree and has a woody flavour. The one on the table is 13 years old.

Down the alley by the side of the house, past clucking chickens, is the village bakery in what looks like a shabby shed with, naturally, a vine trailing up its wall and a washing line for the lengths of cloth in which the bread is wrapped to keep it fresh. Two women are baking tomorrow's batch of wafer-bread which is thin, flat, circular and about a foot in diameter. The fire is kindled with walnut shells and in the oven to one side the second stage of the baking is proceeding. In the first stage, the dough pancake is lightly cooked and then separated into two thinner sections; it is these thin pancakes which are being cooked, one by one, for one minute only. The wafer is then handed to the assistant who has a cork mat slightly larger than the wafer-bread. She stacks them on this mat, pressing down the pile with another mat on top. We all nibble bread and cheese as we watch.

Then it is back to the house to see the shawls for the national costumes being made. An expert can complete the job in 28 days, in two stages. In the first, the plain black silk fringed square is exquisitely embroidered in one corner with flowers and leaves in various colours. Then gold and silver thread and pearls or coral are overlaid on to the existing embroidery. Oliena's costumes are among the finest in Sardinia and with this sort of workmanship it is not difficult to see why.

The seamstresses hand me a bunch of roses and grandmother, seated on a stool in the corner, wishes me 'many more years', the traditional Sard goodbye. The final stop on this charming tour is the local hall, to see pictures of the protected eagles who live in the Sopramonte moun-

tains which back on to the little town and look deceptive-
ly easy to scale. For some unexplained reason an accor-
dionist turns up, there is more wine, and the entire five
strong tourist association breaks into a complicated pagan
dance called S'Arcui, expertly done. Before returning to
Nuoro there is a welcome black coffee at a smart restaurant a few miles up the valley called Su Cologne, after
the river here which is fed by underground streams with,
somewhere up in the mountains, the largest cave in Italy,
$3\frac{1}{2}$ miles long.

It is possible to continue on a rough track from Oliena
to Orgosolo, but a better route is along the valley of the
River de Locoe. The trip is only 30 minutes – and takes
you centuries back in time. The first sinister impression is
of a Wild West town, with my escorts and I taking the
roles of the 'baddies' riding in! The shutters and doors
close, the inhabitants disappear and even the bakery tem-
porarily shuts up shop against the strangers. The reason
is that the town is famed for its vendettas and banditry,
so any foreigner is automatically assumed to be the
enemy and associated with the police, guns, shooting and
death.

Once over this hurdle, by the simple act of collecting
the proprietor of the only hotel to smooth the way, the
wariness and mistrust eases immediately, although it has
not been directed at the obvious alien woman but at the
representatives of the Nuoro tourist board who, because
they come from a city and could be Italians, are suspect.
It is to their credit that they take pains to explain this
aspect of their province and refuse to be worried by the
early animosity of Orgosolo's inhabitants. At the third
try, the bakery opens its doors, news spreads from here of
the identities and purpose of the visitors and from then
on everyone tries to outdo the others in welcome and
hospitality.

It is very quickly clear that you should fast before
arriving. The baker hands over two cartons of sponge
fingers, enough to feed a hungry children's party and at
the shop which sells, among other items, model buildings
made from used matches by the local prisoners, the
shop-keeper presents a record of a traditional Sard sing-

ing group of which he is a member. The two escorts are
needed to help carry the loot. They themselves had begun
the day by giving me a gigantic and magnificent colour
poster of one of their special festivals, and now they have
to carry that, two bottles of wine from Oliena (a third
will be added at lunchtime), the cake boxes, the record
and the flowers; it is about par for the course in a morning of Sardinian visiting.

Orgosolo is a maze of narrow streets, some no wider
than alleyways, and many of the houses bear the DDT
inscription of the post-war malaria eradication campaign.
It is a custom to keep the firewood on the roof and
should space run out stack the remaining logs down the
outside staircase. Some of the tiny terraced houses look
from the street as though they must be one-room dwellings, but picking one at random to visit, and stepping
down into the parlour with its tiled floor, the house
expands. Leading off to one side is the main bedroom,
with a beautiful chest of drawers alongside a cardboard
wardrobe. Sausages and hams are hanging up here and
there is a row of cheeses on the floor, which accounts for
the pungent smell. On the other side of the parlour is the
family living-room, overlooking a little yard. There is running water and a modern stove in the kitchen.

The prevailing 'decorations' throughout the town are
political murals painted in bold colours and on every
spare wall. They are pro-communist and anti-fascist and
anti-nazi and seem to have been done by the same
school-teacher responsible for the bright town scenes that
hang in the dining room of the only hotel. There are oil-
cloths on the tables, but the rush-bottomed chairs have
fine carved backs, and the meal is of a very high standard indeed, the proprietor pointing out that with the
exception of the first course, proscuitto, we are eating
exactly the same as the guests staying here. It is rather
difficult to identify the wine as it has been decanted into
mineral water bottles.

With the ham comes a rather sweet rosé, then the
strong Nero is brought out for the remainder of the meal.
Ravioli is the next course, stuffed with chopped spinach
and a tomato and cheese sauce, then peppery veal

kebabs, then sebada, a pancake sugared on the outside and a cheesey innard. We finish off with a powerful colourless schnapps. There is one final stop to be made in Orgosolo, at the local café to say goodbye over a cup of coffee to all the people we have met that day, then comes the drive down from nearly 2000 feet to the valley, with Nuoro and its Monte Ortobene backcloth on the other side.

The main exit south from the city runs through oak and poplar trees, little apple orchards and a ground cover of rock rose, wild fennel and the dwarf palm whose leaves produce the baskets and whose flower is a delicate lilac and white. The scenery becomes heavily wooded with sections reserved for hunting near Mamoiada, an appropriate pastime because this village is the one that supplies the mamuthones (representing hunted animals) for Sassari's Cavalcata. The inhabitants believe that this character has been around for 1000 years and that the name is Saracen.

There is nothing particularly ancient about the costume, and each year the mamuthones have a new set of bells to carry on their backs and a new mask to hold in front of their faces. The mask is made from pear-tree wood with the outside blackened, and the sculptor makes them, seated on a cork stool, in his kitchen. Mamoiada is largely a sheep-rearing community and as well as 'exporting' their mamuthones to Sassari's festival, they have one of their own in which bonfires are lit and a special cake is baked for guests.

Climbing by road 1000 feet from here, the oak, chestnut and walnut trees become more sparse and the terrain flattens into a plateau before reaching Fonni, the highest village in Sardinia which, with its grey granite houses and moor-like surroundings, looks like a settlement in Scotland. In mid-May there is still snow on the slopes of nearby Monte Spada and sometimes it lasts until the first Sunday in June when there is a festival at the little country church of Our Lady in the Snow. Fonni, together with the other mountain villages of Aritzo, Belvi, Tonara and Desulo, is a place from where the shepherds drive their flocks to the plains of the Campidano in November, to return to their upland pastures in May, snow permitting.

From here you are above the tree line, and it is a windy, cold day at the isolated sporting club, (actually a hotel despite its name) which is a ski-ing centre in winter – the slopes of Bruncu Spina with its lift almost to the summit is four miles away – and in summer goes in for horse riding, tennis and swimming. All year round the hotel takes guests on photographic safaris to see the protected moufflon that survive up here. There is a narrow gulley down which the animals are persuaded to come by beaters, for the benefit of the tourists waiting with their cameras at the bottom. In case you should miss this, the hotel has a mini-zoo in its grounds, in which the star turn is a tame cigarette-munching male moufflon.

Most of the guests on my visit are a group of scientists from NATO countries having a conference on plant diseases. They chose Sardinia not for its diseased plants, but because they hoped it would be warm, and are now shivering their way into the bus. Strangely, at this height and in this area, grows a plant which has largely disappeared from the European scene and is used for heart diseases. A few hundred yards down the track from the hotel, is the spring of clear water with thermal properties available to anyone who happens past.

Between here and Desulo the scenery gets more desolate, the jangle of sheep-bells receding until there is only an occasional cottage with a steep cultivated slope below it and surrounded by enormous holly trees which are a protected species.Up to the pass of S'Arcude Tascussi there are lots of chestnut trees, the nuts of which are sold all over the island, as well as being made into a sort of marmalade chestnut purée. On the other side of the pass the trees are hazel, and a couple of pigs are wandering along the road, which is exactly what you would expect from Desulo, as the village was originally three separate communities started by three families breeding respectively pigs, sheep and cattle.

The last man to wear national costume daily here died four years ago, but on Sunday afternoon the women are wearing theirs and it is unlike other island costumes, because it has a bright orange embroidered Dutch bonnet. Desulo is not quite as high as Fonni, but has the distinction of sitting at the foot of the highest mountain in Sardinia, Punta La Marmora, at 6017 feet, and named after the nineteenth-century Italian statesman and explorer. The village specialises in wooden carvings, some of which, like spoons and dishes, are strung over the balconies of the little houses, reputed to contain the central stone hearths that Sardinia's nuraghic people used.

Today's inhabitants are renowned for their longevity; 90-plus years is by no means rare and they attribute it not to the cool mountain climate and lack of malaria, but, charmingly, to their wine. From Desulo the road begins to drop via winding hairpin bends, each bend with its little vine patch, and near the junction with the N295 there is pine afforestation and the road and railway snake cosily together. If you turn right here, to cut short the excursion, you will be in Tonara in four miles, the place to buy the nougat called Torrone. Turn left and five miles south is the resort of Aritzo, whose menfolk, like those of Desulo, have curious wide-set eyes almost like Lapps.

Walnut and chestnut trees are everywhere and in the old days they made bread from acorns. Now the kitchen is geared to the tourist who has no need to order mineral water as the stuff that comes from the tap is fresh mountain water. Menus feature roast sucking pig, a delicacy the Romans adored, (importing to Italy large numbers of them), usually preceded by a pasta or proscuitto. From Aritzo the road climbs to the Cantoniera Ortuabis, at 2400 feet, and shortly afterwards divides, the left-hand branch taking you to Villanova Tulo and thence to Seui, and the right-hand one with the railway constantly crossing the road, dropping down into Laconi.

This village, in the wooden region of Sarcidano, is the birth-place of St Ignacius, considered to be the St. Francis of Assisi of Sardinia, and it has the Castle of the Marchesi Aymerich. If you continue on south via Nurallao, you will leave the Province of Nuoro shortly after Isili, famed for its rugs and copper work. But to stay up in the mountains, retrace the journey as far as Cantoniera Ortuabis and, instead of branching right to Aritzo, go left and drive through the Barbagia Belvi region, to reach Meana Sardo with its sixteenth-century Aragonese-gothic church of S. Bartolomeo and nearby nuraghe Maria Incatada.

A few miles further on is Atzara and the road continues rising as it has done since Laconi, to bring you into Sorgono, a village with a reputation for honesty and independence – they virtually ruled themselves until the establishment of the House of Savoy. It is the principal village of the Mandrolisai region and has two churches of interest in the vicinity, the sixteenth-century San Mauro with a fine rose window and another church of the same date, the Aragonese-gothic Virgin of Itria. But perhaps the village is best known for D. H. Lawrence's description of his visit in the 1920s.

Only a short distance from Sorgono, turn left to the artificial lake of Gusana made 15 years ago from the damming of the River Taloro stocked with trout, though fishing is permitted only from its banks. To carry on past the lake will bring you back to Fonni, but a different and interesting route is to Gavoi, centre of the Barbagia Ollolai region.

There are about 2000 inhabitants in the little town, but something over 60,000 shepherds in the neighbourhood, and it is a handful of these I am to meet, guided by two young smart French-speaking school-teachers, one of whom is standing for mayor in the forthcoming local elections. The dirt road is a bumpy four miles in glowering stormy weather to the hamlet of Lodine, with its one street and one-storey houses and an almost continuous line of washing that stretches indiscriminately across doors and windows.

A mile out of the hamlet we turn across a field to pull up at a square, granite one-room house with a pack of barking dogs outside. On the door are carved the initials of the shepherds who have lived here, and the current occupiers of 11 years' standing are two brothers who migrate twice a year with their flocks to the plains, in order to take advantage of the two grass crops, both up

here and down there. Shepherds' sons used to join this
trek when they were nine; now, and this is said with
some pride by the teachers, they stay at school for
another two years.

Wives remain in the villages, but the menfolk whose
land is not too far away do get home during the spring
and autumn months they spend in their mountain
pastures. Each man may be only a few hundred yards
from his neighbour, but they work and live alone. By
now it is beginning to rain and the crowd inside the little
house is considerable, 11 all told, five of whom are shepherds and have been working since early morning to
prepare a traditional meal, admittedly on a more extrava-
gant scale than they would normally eat at a sitting.

All attention is focused on the fireplace, which takes up
almost the length of one wall, and the fire is kept burning by propping the logs into an enormous stump of
wood at the back. On either side are stones supporting
the spit on which a young lamb laced with thyme is
roasting, its skin, hanging up on a nail near the door,
indicating that it was killed that morning. One man alone
is responsible for this part of the meal and he has a knife
with a cow-horn handle. In the ashes of the fire is the
stuffed stomach of a sheep and a second cook, seating
like the other man on a rough cork stool, is turning this
object and occasionally lifting it to shake it close to his
ear to judge whether its interior consistency is solid and
therefore done.

Above the fireplace hang wooden trays for smoking the
cheeses. Meanwhile the hors d'oeuvres is yoghourt and
wafer-bread and white wine.The table, for reasons which
will become clear later, is firm, flat and well-made; the
rest of the furnishings have a home-made appearance and
when it is discovered that there are insufficient cork stools
an extra seat is made by fetching a tree stump. Most of
the walls, blackened by smoke, and all the stone floor
space is taken up with the shepherds' tools. The shelving
runs up to the ceiling and our host has to use a long
stick to rake down the cork serving platters stored on the
top shelf. A wooden chest contains the finished cheeses; a
copper cauldron has the pigs' swill; there is butter-mak-

ing machinery and milk churns; water is kept in terracotta urns the shape of Greek amphora.

Each hook on the walls, and there are many of them, has a specific purpose and the occupants are excellent housekeepers, with everything in its place and a place for everything, even down to the safety touch of always putting the knife blade in a cork stopper when it is not in use. The table setting is very simple, just a pile of wafer-bread from a wooden bin in the corner and a salt-cellar the size and shape of a mug and made, naturally, of cork. As the downpour increases in density, the shutters to the only glassless window are closed, the door is propped slightly ajar to get rid of some of the smoke and the gas mantle lit in the now-darkened room. The meal begins with the sheep's stomach, ashes neatly brushed off, to be followed by the intestines which have been cooked in a frying pan and are obviously something of a delicacy, as my host picks out the best bits and hands them to me on the end of his knife.

The next dish is a gigantic mutton stew which has been sitting in an enormous saucepan. The liquid is strained before the contents are upturned into the largest cork platter, a couple of feet long, and so lopsided that a prop is needed to hold it in position. The shepherd who tucks the salt cellar under one end to serve this purpose is gently reprimanded by the host, who points out that the salt will be needed and sends out for a small log which does admirably. The stew has onions, leeks and potatoes, and it is this latter vegetable which is the luxury, not the meat, for the cultivation of potatoes is dying out and except in the smartest hotels they do not appear on menus.

Finally, we come to the kid itself, which the host carves into lumps with his knife and hands around. To complete the banquet are the cheeses, one resembling Stilton and the other the hard-as-nails type, produced from a soft goatskin rucksack hanging on a hook by the door. Another two-litre bottle of red wine appears and we shift round slightly to avoid the leaks in the roof. The most junior shepherd is deputed to clear away, industriously sweeping the floor beneath our feet, and the others arrange themselves in a line on the bed for a sing-song, only the leader of the quartet actually singing the dirge-like Sardinian religious chants, while the others make a kind of growling noise.

Come 4 p.m., rain or no, the two brothers have to milk the sheep and I am clad, like them, in yellow oil-skins, complete with 'lifeboat' style hat and Charlie Chaplin rubber boots. The donkey, whose saddle has been slung over a tree branch outside the house, has been taken up the hill with four large milk churns and a couple of smaller ones, and we trudge off after the animal. The sheep-pen, a rough corral of brushwood, is entirely empty and the flock are scattered over the hillside. There are no sheep-dogs, surprising in the light of the barkers who greeted our arrival, and the sheep are herded into the pen by a combination of whistles, shouts and throwing stones in which I am involved, simply because I am wearing clothes the animals will recognise. I am strategically positioned and wave my arms and shout with the best.

This haphazard system succeeds in about 15 minutes and is assured once the ram with his fine bell is persuaded into the pen. The shepherds take about 1½ hours to milk 330 sheep with a yield of 120-140 litres, and back at the house the talk turns to politics, as it often does in this mountain province. The discussion is an animated one, for the shepherds are a vehement and articulate group, and it would seem that the school-teacher, with fairly leftish views, will succeed in his first bid for mayor. The conversation is broken off by the return of the laden donkey, the calling of the pigs to eat their food, served in a trough that is half a lorry tyre, and the next vital stage of the work, which must be done immediately and speedily.

A copper cauldron is put on a tripod over the fire, and the steaming contents of the churns poured into it. A thermometer lets the cheese-makers know when the temperature reaches the required 55°F and the milk is given an occasional stir with an implement the size of a garden hoe. After a quarter of an hour the cauldron is removed from the fire and placed on a rubber tyre. There is a lit-

tle more stirring, including the addition of a sour ingred-
ient, then a wooden frame is put over the top and
covered with a black wool cloth.

The lunch table is scrubbed down and now the banquet has
been cleared its special construction can be noted: a thin rim
on three sides and a diamond point at one end to provide a
run-off. It is now 6 p.m. and 20 minutes after the churns arrived at the house, the milk is turning into cheese. The two
brothers remove the frame and cloth, roll up their sleeves and,
seated on either side, plunge their arms to the bottom of the
cauldron to squeeze together the fast-forming solid mass. This
requires muscle and speed. The wooden frame is replaced and
on it are put the cheese moulds.

By this time, the unseen bottom is so solid that it
requires a knife to slice it into manageable sections, so
that it can be scooped out by hand and pressed into the
moulds, the surplus liquid escaping through holes in the
bottom. Eventually each mould is an overflowing pudding
filled with cottage cheese, when it is smartly flipped over
so that the smooth side is uppermost, and pressed down
all over again with yet more cheese added. When it is
clear that no more can be crammed in, the moulds are
removed to the table where the same process goes on, the
superfluous liquid running out of the diamond point into
a bucket.

A third shepherd joins the team to work at the table
and the game of 'sand castles' proceeds while the milk
level in the cauldron drops dramatically. Five moulds,
each of five kilos, is the evening production, all for
export, the remainder of the milk being either drunk or
turned into butter, and the whole process will be repeated
at 6 a.m. Once the moulds are nearly ready there is a
brief supper break of yoghourt, cold stew and the remains
of the roast lamb, then a final few squeezes and the
moulds are left on the table overnight. The next day they
will join the ones already in the wooden cheese chest for
48 hours, making them ready for market. The fire is
damped down, the little cottage shut, the dogs left on
guard and the shepherds drive back to town for what
remains of the evening and to continue the political discussion.

The main road north from Gavoi remains at an altitude of around 2000 feet for the ten miles to Sarule, where they make the carpets seen in the permanent exhibition in Sassari. The village shares with its neighbour, Orani, a nine-day festival similar to the one at Lula, each taking turns to organize the event at the church of Nostra Signora di Gonari, which sits in the hills about equidistant between the villages. Orani is famous for its costumes and has the nearby Pisan-romanesque church of S. Paolo. The last settlement on this road is Oniferi outside which, close to the road, is the Domus de Janas Sas Concas, a most sinister row of holes in a low rock face surrounded by prickly pears. Not for the first time the term giant's tomb for these strange constructions seems a misnomer, when an ordinary mortal cannot even enter one of the tiny chambers.

Nuoro is only a few minutes' drive, and to explore the remaining wedge of the province and its eastern coastline requires an overnight stop at or near the shore. Heading eastwards from the capital there are the now familiar olive groves before the countryside becomes wilder. After 12 miles there is a turn-off towards Dorgali across a flat plateau and the signpost to Serra Orrios, the site of one of the most important nuraghic villages in Sardinia, where excavations in 1936 revealed 70 or so round-hut dwellings, a common well and a stone central hearth called Domu de su Fumu.

The sign points through an open gate and up a gravel track, depositing the disconcerted traveller in an amiable farmyard. Not for the first time the splendid exhortations to visit something or other have gone awry. The chickens are scratching about beneath the olive trees and a path leads away from the yard, clearly to the ruin. A friendly dog with a piece of corrugated iron for a sofa wags a tail, then there is a crude brush fence across the path and a fearful barking from a sheepdog a few hundred yards away, who is guarding not only his flock, but Serra Orrios, too. Just to point up the difficulty, the low stone farm field walls have an extra defensive layer of brushwood on top, all of which obviously keeps the animals in their places and has the same effect for humans.

There is nothing else to do except continue the journey, crossing a fine high bridge over the River Cedrino, with the original low-slung stone one alongside, then into Dorgali, with the wall of the 2500-foot Monte Bardia behind it. This town was a Saracen settlement and has a cluster of little-known archaeological sights around it, including a very strange retreat at nearby Monte Tiscali, believed to have been occupied during the Roman period by rebellious Sards, who rightly felt safe in their cave hideaway.

Twentieth-century Dorgali concerns itself with ceramics, terracotta, rugs and leather work, most of the shops dealing in one or other of these items; but at this particular moment it is also a town of concrete mixers and brick lorries and what is not actually being built or demolished is fairly modern, with only a hint of the original grey granite houses in the back streets. To leave the province, head north to Orosei, the village which the Romans called Fanum Carisii, at the mouth of the Cedrino with a fertile stretch between sea and mountains. There is a fine old tower, part of the mediaeval castle, and from the Piazza del Popolo a steep flight of steps leads to the Primiziale church, which seems to have expanded into three quite separate sections, all of which are bolted and barred as are the two other churches within a few hundred yards of the piazza.

The estuary fertility is short-lived and the rocky hills crowd in until about 12 miles south of Siniscola, when the cornfields and pine trees appear on the alluvial plain formed by the River Siniscola. There was a prehistoric settlement in the area and today the town is a bustling agricultural centre whose houses have their own vines and lemon trees in the gardens. The altar of the sixteenth-century San Giovanni was being rebuilt on my visit, but the rest of the church is a good example of baroque, with ceiling frescoes and half-marble pillars. The road now hugs the coast and just before crossing the Posada River is the twelfth-century Castle of Fava, with its tall towers and battlements looking very imposing as there are no nearby buildings. It is the last sight before crossing the provincial border and entering Sassari Province.

But you should double-back south, for near Dorgali is one of the great sights of Sardinia, reached by a four-mile stretch of road that turns almost straight into a tunnel, where the other traffic is a herd of pigs followed by a donkey and a swineherd. The other side drops down in sharp curves to the little port and resort of Cala Gonone. The sea is calm, so the trip to the famous Grotta del Bue Marino is possible, and on an off-season morning there are about 15 customers of varying ages and nationalities.

For the major part of the journey south from the port, the boat sticks close to the shore with its rocky fringe and macchia-covered cliff hiding the hinterland from view. The cliff has lots of little caves and one particularly sinister one which is reached by a ladder down the cliff-face, with a rough wooden handrail to stop the intrepid falling into the ocean. The road, looking like a narrow ledge, stops here, and though there are plans to extend it the extra three miles to the grotto, it will be a difficult and expensive job, given the terrain.

Just under half an hour after leaving the harbour the boat sneaks into an opening and moors at a concrete jetty in about four feet of water. The tour of the grotto – it has been open to tourists for 20 years – takes one hour and is unique in two respects: it is dry, so no slimy slippery walls and walkways; and it is hot, instead of the more usual clammy fustiness associated with caves. The guide, who travels with the trippers, fetches a lantern and goes ahead with this giant gas lighter to ignite flares along the route, and on our return the boatman comes behind to switch them off. Each of the dozens of flares has its own cylinder and it would seem to be a most practical and economical arrangement, though whether the gas would have any long-term effect on the rock formations only a geologist could tell.

At first the walkway stays near the water's edge, with charming arches and tiny caves and a cavernous hall they call the ballroom. Then the route heads inland and crosses a little bridge where one side has sea water and the other fresh, in a small pretty chamber where the stalactites are still in the first stages of infancy. You need to watch your head through the tunnels, and down a short flight of steps is a larger hall with a ceiling of coral and a whole wall of lacy stalactites in pinks, whites, creams and browns. Suddenly, there is sand underfoot and the tour emerges briefly into a rocky inlet where surely mermaids must ride in on the backs of the seals that live here. The species is called Monachus Albiventer, survives from the Ice Age and are the only seals still found in the Mediterranean. Alas, neither they nor mermaids are visible today.

One of the strangest constructions at this point reveals a cave below the one the visitors are standing in, so that their feet are on its ceiling and they can look over into it. The path now leads away into the interior, to a dramatic area where there are deep rifts in the rock face and a formation they call Dante, after a fancied resemblance to the man, all in much darker tones. The next gallery should be named after a modern art museum, for scattered about its wavy sandy floor are rocks precisely like modern sculpture.

Anything that has even the slightest recognizable appearance has been named accordingly. A phalanx of stalactites is called the organ and there is another formation entitled the wedding cake. The guide is a jolly fellow who, though he must have done this a thousand times, clearly loves his grotto and imparts his enthusiasm to the trippers who make a happy chatting group on the quicker return trip to Cala Gonone, where it is lunchtime and an opportunity to sample one of the restaurants that are clustered around the harbour and the small beach.

Sea bream is the most popular choice, cooked with herbs and a hint of garlic, in a trattoria with a giant turtle shell on the wall, the turtle having been caught here. The young waiter obviously wants to go out and catch another one and to aid him he has bought a fish-finder made in Japan for his boat. The instruction manual is in English and he confidently hands it to me for translation into Italian. I dare not tell the lad that I do not understand the instructions in my own language, much less being able to put them into another.

There is only one way out of Cala Gonone, and that is back up the cliff road past the increasing villa development and through the tunnel to rejoin the road going south where, in just over ten miles, it rises to the pass of Genna Silana, around 3000 feet, and then drops down past Urzulei to the little village of Baunei, overlooking the valley of the River Pramaera. Just before you reach that river estuary there is a detour to be made off the main road a couple of miles to Santa Maria Navarrese with its picturesque tower, beach and eleventh-century church built by the daughter of the King of Navarre who was shipwrecked here.

A welter of river deltas all meet nearby and on the banks of the River Mirenu is the Castle of Medusa. The road runs past the Stagno di Tortoli and a short while further on is the town of Tortoli which has yet another river, the Roddeddu, making the whole area a very watery one indeed, so there are lush vineyards and orchards and banana plantations. Tortoli was the ancient capital of the Quirra, there are several nuraghe in the vicinity and by the seashore is Arbatax, famous for its red cliffs and pink sand beaches.

The granite houses stretch along the headland and most of the inhabitants are connected with fishing, the ports and its ferry service to Olbia and Genoa, or the railway, this being the end of the line from Cagliari on this side of the island. Its exposed position must have made the nearby Torre S. Gemiliano rather important in earlier days. These towers, built by the Spaniards against African pirates, were later converted into customs look-out posts, the idea being that the watchmen inside would catch smugglers. As the former were easily bribed with a basket of fruit, a sheep or a skin of wine, all beyond their meagre salaries, the system did not work too well.

But as defence points they were in use as late as 1812, when the Torre S. Giovanni di Sarrala about 20 miles south of Arbatax, was the scene of a victory by the Ogliastrini against the Corsairs. It would be sensible to spend a night in this region of Ogliastra with its limestone hills, perhaps at Arbatax, in order to explore further by a convenient circular route. From Tortoli go south to Bari Sardo, which sits in a positive nest of nuraghe interspersed with vineyards and almond groves and which has in its parish church a copy of Raphael's 'Holy Family' by the Sard painter Antioco Mainas.

Continue on south for about ten miles, crossing or running alongside several rivers, and then branch off to Ierzu which makes excellent rosé wine and has many unexplored caves. The road rises to Ulassai, then begins to drop until you turn left at a junction to drive into the region of Barbagia Seulo and through Ussassai to the pass of Monte Arqueri at over 3000 feet. The other side drops down into Seui and the road sticks closely to the railway line, passing the top end of the Flumendosa lake, of which there are two, so do not think your map-reading has gone wrong. This route will enable you to reach Cagliari.

To stay in Nuoro Province retrace the few miles back to the junction and carry on up a snaky road to Gairo where a new village has been built to replace the one that was slipping into the River Pardu. One more cross-roads and one more decision: turn left alongside the River Sicarderba to the high Flumendosa lake three miles away; or right to Lanusei, the principal centre of the region and the place to sample Shakespeare's Malmsey which is called Malvasia here. There could hardly be a more fitting conclusion to a Sardinian holiday than to be musing over the mediaeval characteristics the island presents with its costumes and festivals, while quaffing a mediaeval draft.

Index

Abbasanta 89, 90
Acquafredda castle 77
Aga Khan 121
Aggius 117
Airports 19
Aix-la-Chapelle, Treaty of, 17
Ales 89
Alghero 9, 15, 16, 28, 105-108
Altopiano Abbasanta plain 90
Antas river 78
Aragonese 15, 76, 81, 82, 83
Arbatax 19, 119, 164
Arborea 88
Arbus 78
Ardara 115
Ardauli 89
Aritzo 26
Arzachena 122
Asinara 104
Assemini 25
Atzara 26, 27

Bari Sardo 164
Baronia 29
Barumela castle 89
Barumini 58-60
Belvi 152
Bessude 110
Bidighinzu lake 110
Bitti 29
Bolotana 148
Bonarcado 91
Bono 27, 116
Bonorva 110
Borutta 110
Bosa 145
Brancaleone Doria 82, 83, 84
Burgos 116
Busachi 27, 89
Byzantines 14, 15

Cabras 28, 34, 81, 92
Cagliari, city, 11, 13, 14, 16, 19, 23, 27, 30, 31, 39-55, 83, 92, 96, 99, 101, 106, 110, 139, 147, 164
   Archbishop's Palace 43
   Castello district 39
   Castello San Michele 49, 50
   Governor's Palace 43
   Grotto of the Viper 48, 49
   National Archaeological Museum 43-46, 147
   Palazzo Communale 52
   Piazza Palazzo 41
   Poetto 53
   Roman Amphitheatre 50, 51
   San Saturnino 47, 48
   San Cecilia Cathedral 41–42
   San Domenico, church 54
   St. Remy Bastion 3)
   Stagno di S. Gilla 53
   Tower of the Elephants 40
   University 40
Cagliari, province 56-79
Cala Gonone 162, 163
Cala Regina 64
Calangianus 118
Calasetta 72

Campidano Minove 88
Campidano, plain of 29, 56, 57, 152
Cap Caccia 109
Cap Falcone 104
Cap San Marco 93
Capitana 64
Capo Boi 64
Capo Carbonara 64
Caprera island 131-136
Capula, Giovanni 40
Car ferries 19, 20
Carbonia 75
Carlo Emanuele III, King of Sardinia, 16, 17, 72, 73
Carloforte 72, 73
Carta di Logu 83, 84
Carthaginians 11, 13, 14, 59, 68, 70, 75, 92, 118, 119, 140, 145
Castel Sardo 111-112, 118, 136, 137
Castello S. Michele 49, 50
Cavalcata Sarda, festival of, 30-35
Cavoli 64
Cellini, Benvenuto 42
Cicero 14, 48
Coghinas lake 116
Collinas 29
Coltellazzo, tower 68
Cornus 92
Corsi Mascherati festival 116
Costa del Sud 69
Costa Smeralda 10, 19, 120-125
Costa Verde 78
Cuglieri 92

David, Gerard 42
Decimomannu 19
Deledda, Grazia 141-42
Desulo 27, 29, 153-54
Dolianova 62
Domus de Janas 13
Domus de Maria 69
Domus de Janas Sant'Andrea Priu 110
Domusnovas 77, 78
Don Alphonso, Infante 76
Don Martino 57
Dona Teresa 78
Dorgali 58

Eleanora d'Arborea 80, 82-84
Elmas 19, 29

Fava castle 161
Feast of the Grapes 72
Feast of the Redemption 143
Felice, Carlo 43
Fertilia 109
Fertilia, airport 19
Festivals 12, 22-38
   Cavalcata Sarda 30-36, 96, 152
   Corsi Mascherati 116
   Feast of the Grapes, Calasetta 72
   Feast of the Redemption 143
   Our Lady in the Snow 152
   S'Ardia di San Constantino 90
   Sa Sartiglia 86
   Sagra di Sant'Efisio 23, 24
   San Francesco 36

Filindeu bread 36
Flumendosa, river 63
Fluminimaggiore 78
Fonni 152, 154, 155
Fonte Renaggin 117
Fordongianus 89

Gairo 165
Galassi, Andrea 42
Garibaldi, Giuseppe 131-35
Gavoi 155-59
Gennargentu mountains 144
Genoese 11, 15, 72, 81, 83, 118
Geremeas 64
Gherardesca family 75
　Guelfo della 77, 91
　Ugolino della 77, 91
Ghilarza 89, 90
Giant's Tombs 13
Giara di Gesturi 60, 89
Goceano mountains 116
　castle 116
Golfo Aranci 120
Goths 14
Gremi 32
Grotta de su Coloru 113
Grotta del Bue Marino 162
Grotta di Nettuno 109
Grotto of S. Giovanni 77
Grotto of the Viper 48, 49
Gulf of Oristano 88
Gusana, lake 155
Guspini 78

Ierzu 165
Iglesias 26, 75-77, 78
Isili 154
Ittiri 26, 27

Jesuits 16
Jews 14, 16, 138

La Caletta 75
La Maddalena 20, 125
La Maddalena di Rimedio church 90
La Pelosa 103
La Punta 75
Laconi 154
Laerru 113
Lanusei 165
Lawrence, D. H. 41, 155
Limbara mountains 116
Locoe river 150
Logudorese 11
Lombards 15
Losa, nuraghe 90
Lula, festival at 36

Macomer 147
Mamoiada 33
Mamuthones 33, 34
Mandas 60
Mannu river 91
Mariano IV, Giudice of Arborea 81, 82
Marina di Torre Grande 92
Marmilla region 89
Martin II of Aragon 41
Meano Sardo 155
Milis 91
Milis Pizzinu church 91
Miliziani 29
Mogoro 28
Molara island 120

Monastir 57
Monreale castle 78
Monte Arci 88
Monte Ferru castle 91
Monte Pranu, lake 70
Monteleone Rocca Doria 109
Monteponi lake 78
Montevecchio 78
Moor's Watch Tower 75
Morgongiori 89
Muravera 63
Murra 38

Napoleon 17, 125
Nelson, Horatio Lord 125-30
Neoneli 89
Nero wine 148-49
Nora 29, 67, 68
Norris, Admiral 119
Nuoro 11, 138-143
　Cathedral 142
　Costume Museum 142
　Feast of the Redemption 143
　Province 144-65
Nulvi 113
Nuraghe 13, 88, 89, 90, 110, 155
Nurallao 154
Nuraminis 57

Olbia 19, 118, 119
Oliena 148
Ollolai 35
Omodeo lake 89
Orani 160
Orgosolo 27, 28, 150-52
Oristano 11, 78, 80-86
　Cathedral 85
　Palazzo Communale 85
　Sa Sartiglia festival 86
　San Francesco church 85
　Santa Chiara church 85
　Seminario Tridentino 85
　Torre Portixedda 85
　Torre San Cristoforo 85
Oristano province 87-93
Orosei 161
Orune 139
Oschiri 116
Osilo 27, 113
Ozieri 115

Palau 125
Palmas river 70
Paulilatino 90
Pattaoa 116
Pearce, Benjamin 147-8
Phoenicians 13, 39, 68, 75
Piedmont 16, 17
Pirri 26
Pisans 11, 15, 81, 118, 137
Ploaghe 114
Poetto 53
Porto Cervo 122
Porto di Teulada 69
Porto S. Paulo 119-20
Porto Torres 19, 94, 97, 99, 101-3, 104, 111,
　114, 147
Portoscuso 75
Portovesme 72, 75
Pozzomaggiore 109
Pula 68
Punta Gennarta, lake 78

Quarto Sant'Elena 27, 64, 65
Quirra, castle 63

Rais 73
Reni, Guido 42
Romans, 9, 10, 14, 15, 45, 46, 59, 68, 70, 72
  79, 89, 92, 101, 102, 118

S'Ardia di San Constantino festival 90
S. Efisio 27, 30
Sa Sartiglia festival 86
Sagra di San'Efisio, festival 23, 24, 30
Salto di Quirra 63
San Angelo 78
San Gavino cathedral 102, 103
San Gavino Monreale 78
San Giovanni de Sinis church 93
San Leonardo de Siete Fuentes church 91
San Lussurgiu church 89
San Michele di Salvenero church 114
San Nicola church 78
San Nicolo di Trullus church 110
San Palermo church 90
San Pietro 20, 28, 72, 73
San Pietro Extramuros church 146
San Salavatore church 93
San Saturnino, basilica 47, 48
San Simplicio church 119
San Vero Milis 26, 90
Sandalieta 13
Sanguinaccio 37
Sanluri 29
Sant'Antioco 20, 70, 71, 72
Sant'Antioco di Bisarcio church 115
Santa Caterina di Pittinuri
Santa Lussurgiu 91
Santa Margherita 69
Santa Maria church 91
Santa Maria del Regno church 115
Santa Maria Navarrese 164
Santa Teresa di Gallura 19, 20, 136-37
Santa Trinita di Saccargia church 114
Santadi 26
Saracens 15, 89
Sardara 79
Sardo 11
Sardus 13
Sardus Pata 78
Sarroch 30
Sarule 26, 34, 160
Sassari 11, 94-99
  G. A. Sanna Museum 99
  Music Conservatory 95
  Palazzo Communale 96
  Palazzo della Provincia 95
  Palazzo Giordano 95
  Piazza Cavallino di Honestia 95
  Piazza del Comune 96
  Piazza d'Italia 94
  Piazza Santa Maria 98
  San Francesco church 97
  San Nicola Cathedral 95, 96
  University 96
Sassari province 100-137
Satta, Sebastiano 126

Savoy, House of 16, 18
Sedilo 32, 90
Sedini 113
Sennori 111
Senorbi 60
Serdiana 62
Setti Fratelli mountains 64
Silanis river 113
Siliqua 77
Sinis peninsula 92
Siniscola 161
Sinnai 61, 62
Sirai Hill 75
Solanus 64
Sorgono 155
Sorso 111
Sos Molinos river 91
Spanish 11
  Inquisition 16
Stagno di San Caterina 70
Stagno di S.Gilla 53
Stagno di Santa Giusta 87
Stella Maris church 123
Stintino 103
Su Nuraxi 58
Suelli 60
Sulcis 70, 71

Tavolara island 120
Tegula 69
Tempio Pausanio 116, 117
  Piazza Gallura 117
  Piazza San Pietro
Temple of Antas 78
Term di Sardara 79
Terralba 88
Teulada 29, 69
Tharros 93
Thiesi 110
Tirso river 89
Tonnara 73
Torre di Chia 69
Tortoli 164
Tratalias 70
Truguet, Admiral 73
Turritano 101
Tyndale, John Warre 11, 12, 43, 58, 84

Ula Tirso 89
Ulassai 165
Unification with Italy 18
Uras 88
Urzulei 164
Uri 27
Ussassai 165

Vandals 14, 89
Villa d'Arborea 92
Villa D'Orri 30, 65, 67
Villacidro 78
Villagrande 27
Villanova Monteleone 109
Villasalto 63
Villehermosas family 65-67
Vittorio Amadeo II, King of Sardinia 16